Best Informed Wins

Collected Articles of
Bob Lohfeld from
Washington Technology
2010 – 2012

Edited by Beth Wingate

Best Informed Wins

Collected Articles of
Bob Lohfeld from
Washington Technology
2010 – 2012

Edited by Beth Wingate

©Copyright 2013 Lohfeld Consulting Group, Inc.
All rights reserved.
Articles reprinted with permission from
WashingtonTechnology.com
Printed in United States of America
ISBN: 978-0-9887554-2-0

Published by Lohfeld Consulting Group, Inc.
940 South River Landing Road
Edgewater, Maryland 21037

For more information, contact Info@LohfeldConsulting.com

Production and design: Beth Wingate

While every precaution has been taken in the preparation of this book, the publisher, authors, and editor assume no responsibility for errors or omissions, or for damages resulting from the use of the information contained herein.

Dedication

Many thanks to Nick Wakeman, Editor-in-Chief of *WashingtonTechnology.com* for your years of support and dedication to our government contracting industry.

Best Informed Wins

Collected Articles of Bob Lohfeld from *Washington Technology* **(2010 – 2012)**

Contents

To succeed, deliver what you promised................... 1

Better reviews equal better proposals..................... 5

Get the most out of your contract debriefing 10

5 tips for hiring a proposal consultant 15

3 Steps to improving your proposals...................... 21

What the government won't tell you about your proposal 26

3 Keys to creating winning proposals..................... 31

10 Reasons why you need capture management 36

Resolve to improve your win rate 42

Ask the right questions to understand customer objectives 46

5 Passing grades you need to lead the pack 50

3 Critical steps to surviving tough times 55

Pitfalls to avoid in a down market......................... 60

Best Informed Wins
Collected Articles of Bob Lohfeld from
Washington Technology **(2010 – 2012)**

Why your win rate is hurting your business	65
5 Predictions for the 2020 Market	71
7 tips for crafting a dominant proposal summary	77
6 Ways your proposals fail	82
How bad are your proposals?	88
How to raise your win rate by 20%	92
3 tips to maximize past performance	103
How to avoid a contract protest	108
6 quick fixes that will improve your company's win rate	113
Can you keep your bid out of the reject box?	119
Will low-price contracting make us all losers?	124
100 words that kill your proposals	132
4 Keys to better capture analytics	137
Do's and don'ts of lowering your proposal costs	145
7 steps from good to great proposals	152
Today's market demands benchmarking proposals—here's how	158

Best Informed Wins
Collected Articles of Bob Lohfeld from *Washington Technology* **(2010 – 2012)**

To succeed, deliver what you promised

Contract failures often trace back to poor performance

The victory celebration is almost over, and people are starting to say it's time to get to work on the new contract. All the parties involved have raised their glasses and toasted to the many contributions made by all the players: the business development, capture, and proposal teams. All players deserve a share of the glory that accrues to the winner, and yet there is this nagging feeling that we should put away the champagne glasses and begin preparing to perform the newly awarded contract. For the next five years, it is the operations team that has to carry the ball and fulfill all the promises we made in our proposal.

Best Informed Wins
Collected Articles of Bob Lohfeld from
Washington Technology (2010 – 2012)

Throughout our winning proposal, we made claims about how we would perform the contract if awarded. We bragged about the tools and technology we would use and how we would use those to deliver services that exceed the performance requirements of the contract. We talked about the corporate resources we would make available to the program and subject-matter experts we would shuttle in and out like players on a football team. And, we set high performance standards for ourselves, assuring the customer we would meet, but mostly exceed, the performance requirements in the contract. Many of those claims were viewed as strengths by the evaluation team when they evaluated our proposal, and those strengths contributed to our firm being selected for this contract award.

Now that the award is in place, it is incumbent on our performing team to carry out the many promises and commitments we made. To do this, the performing team needs to build its book of promises into its contract execution plan. Do this systematically, starting with the executive summary of the proposal, which is often rich in commitments and promises, then go to the technical and management volumes of the proposal. Don't forget the other volumes of the proposal because commitments are frequently made in volumes dealing with the transition plan, attached plans that we provided with our proposal, and even the contract volume. List each promise and describe what we committed to do.

Review your book of promises with your new customer and get their buy-in. I've found some commitments made in the proposal were not accepted by the customer and, in fact, were actually down-scored in the proposal. In other procurements, the proposal evaluation was done by an independent team not involved in contract performance. In those instances, the performing organization never saw your proposal or the promises you made. Before implementing your book of promises, make sure the customer concurs with each activity and endorses your plan.

As good project managers, you should manage each commitment as a separate task in your project performance plan. Assign responsibility for accomplishing each task to a specific member of the project team, set the schedule for accomplishing each task, and identify the resources needed. Integrate those activities into your overall project plan and manage those along with your other project activities. Make sure you can report separately how well you are doing on fulfilling your book of promises.

Some government agencies will incorporate your proposal as part of the contract, and some will not. Some agencies might incorporate your promises as a separate page in the contract. When they do, and your proposal is firm fixed price, the promises made are delivered at the bidder's expense. If the bid is cost-plus-fixed-fee, cost-plus-award-fee or cost-plus-incentive-fee, the cost of fulfilling your book of promises might be included in the contract, although that can become contentious.

Whether your customer does or does not incorporate your proposal, it is still your responsibility to deliver on your commitments. Some companies come up short in this regard and forget that promises made in the proposal should be delivered in contract performance. Don't let your company fall into this trap. A promise made is a promise kept.

WashingtonTechnology.com, November 9, 2010

Best Informed Wins
Collected Articles of Bob Lohfeld from *Washington Technology* (2010 – 2012)

Better reviews equal better proposals

A systematic process can raise competitiveness and increase win probability

Independent reviews ensure that proposals are compliant and responsive to the request for proposals. They also guarantee that proposals are feature-rich and technically and politically sound. Reviews should begin early in the proposal process and continue throughout proposal development. Each review builds quality into the proposal. When done well, reviews raise your competitiveness and increase your win probability.

A solid review begins with experienced, knowledgeable reviewers and a comprehensive review plan. Your reviewers should include technical and management experts who deeply understand the subject of your proposal. Be sure to include customer experts who can bring the voice of the customer to your review process. The better your proposal reviewers, the better your review.

Assign sections of the proposal to each reviewer that match his or her areas of expertise. For planning purposes, in a one-day review, assume reviewers can review about 40 pages of the proposal and provide constructive written comments. Assign multiple reviewers, typically three, to each proposal section.

Pick your reviewers carefully. Let them know in advance what section or sections of the proposal they will review and forward the RFP and amendments for them to read before the review.

Each review should begin with a briefing that provides background on the procurement, competition, and strategy. Keep the background information brief and get right into the review schedule and assignments. Detail what you want the reviewers to do. Prescribe the order for each person to review the sections and reinforce what is expected from each reviewer. Review for compliance and responsiveness to the RFP, completeness of features and information, and technical correctness across all sections. Reviewers should not edit the proposals because that happens later in the process.

Document all comments electronically using track changes and insert comments functions, type comments into a separate document, or post them into an electronic template. Your proposal manager should choose the best method for your team.

Consider having reviewers rate the section they review. Color coding is a simple way to summarize how well the section scored: Blue for a well-written, fully compliant response, followed by green, yellow, and red if the section was noncompliant or nonresponsive. Color scores help prioritize proposal rework and give writers some indication of how well they did with their sections.

Some reviewers like to consolidate review comments, and others prefer to let all reviewers present their comments individually. A benefit of the latter would be writers and reviewers could learn from individual comments, and in addition, consolidating comments might be too time-consuming. Gather all electronic comments and load them into your proposal repository for later use.

Conduct the oral debriefing with all writers and reviewers present—virtually or in person. Let each reviewer provide an opening statement summarizing his or her general assessment. Next, debrief reviewer comments section by section, letting each reviewer present significant comments. To keep reviewers from piling on, encourage reviewers to avoid repeating comments previously made by another reviewer.

Manage the review as a debrief—not a debate—and do not let writers challenge or argue about reviewers' comments. After all reviewers have presented their significant comments, ask each to provide closing comments. If managed well, the complete debrief for a 150-page proposal review should last less than two hours.

Review comments are advisory, and the proposal team needs to sort out which are worth heeding. For highly scored sections, writers should feel comfortable accepting or rejecting comments, as they deem appropriate. For sections that scored poorly, writers need to obtain guidance from the proposal manager before making changes. In the color-coded scoring scale, a red section would warrant a revised outline before going forward.

Do not be discouraged if you receive many review comments. The more good comments you get, the better your final proposal will be.

WashingtonTechnology.com, June 28, 2010

Get the most out of your contract debriefing

Be prepared to ask questions and learn as much as possible

Win or lose, you are entitled to receive a debriefing from the government to help you understand the basis for an award decision. You must request your debriefing in writing within three days after receiving notification of contract award, otherwise your request might be declined.

The government will do its best to provide the debriefing within five days of receiving your written request. The debriefing might be done orally, in writing or via another method acceptable to the contracting officer. Most

FREE for Your Board

Here's a way to add spice to your board meeting and it's FREE.

You know David Lansdowne. He's the author of *Fund Raising Realities Every Board Member Must Face* – the second* bestselling fundraising book in history.

Now when you order five or more copies for your board, David will include a FREE set of training activities that highlight the key elements of major gifts fundraising:

- Identifying your key prospects
- Finding the best chair
- Stimulating board giving
- Knowing how much to ask for
- Becoming comfortable with asking

It's a powerful way to engage your board, and each activity is tied to a specific chapter.

Use it and your next board meeting could be the most productive ever.

*Asking, by Jerold Panas (Emerson & Church, Publishers), is number one.

Emerson & Church
PUBLISHERS

Discounts available for quantity purchases.
Call 508-359-0019 or visit www.emersonandchurch.com

bidders prefer oral debriefings because they provide an opportunity to discuss the findings and ask follow-up questions. For some debriefings, travel costs might be a factor, requiring a debriefing through a teleconference. The least-preferable debriefing format, from a learning point of view, is a letter debriefing.

The contracting officer who led the procurement usually leads oral debriefings, supported by the people who participated in the evaluation of proposals. For larger procurements, you can expect government attendees to include technical, management, and past-performance evaluators; cost analysts; and other supporting staff members.

You should ensure that the debriefing team knows you are present to learn so that you can do better on the next proposal. Make it clear that you know this is not the forum to debate or challenge the findings—the government officials also will make that clear.

The government will be well prepared to conduct the debriefing, and you should be, too. To prepare, it's a good idea to reread the request for proposals, questions and answers, RFP amendments, and your proposal. It's also helpful to prepare a list of questions you would like to ask. Don't hesitate to ask follow-up questions so you learn as much as you can about how the government scored your proposal and conducted the evaluation process.

The government is required to provide specific information in the debriefing, including but not limited to:

- The overall cost or price and evaluation rating for your proposal and the winner's proposal.

- The significant weaknesses and deficiencies in your proposal. That often includes your proposal's strengths, although that information is not required.

- Past-performance evaluation results for your proposal, though not the names of people serving as past-performance references.

- The selection rationale and award decision.

You can expect the government to answer reasonable questions about the evaluation results and process. But, the officials won't give you a point-by-point comparison of your proposal with another offeror's proposal, nor will they reveal information considered a trade secret or protected under the Freedom of Information Act.

Because debriefings are intended to be learning exercises, listen carefully. Teams have been surprised to learn that win themes had no effect, and features they thought were compelling were seen as weaknesses and scored as risks. That knowledge is something to take back and rethink for your next effort.

Some companies have learned surprising things in debriefings. Imagine the potential consequences of learning the following in a debriefing.

The weaknesses cited for a proposal actually belonged to another offeror, and the evaluation team mixed up the proposals during the evaluation.

The government ignored its own evaluation criteria and imposed an undisclosed evaluation scheme.

The evaluation criteria specified a relative order of importance for evaluation subfactors, but those were ignored when assessing the relative merits of the proposals.

That information could result in re-evaluation of proposals or filing of protests.

In most cases, you will walk away from a debriefing with an increased understanding of how the government evaluated your proposal and have better insight into what you could have done differently to improve your proposal score.

Some agencies will ask for your thoughts about how the procurement could have been conducted better. Make this a learning opportunity for the government, too. If they did a good job, tell them so.

WashingtonTechnology.com, October 27, 2010

5 tips for hiring a proposal consultant

Additional proposal expertise during the busy season can help boost win rates

Proposal activities in the government market generally peak in the summer months. The requests for proposals that we have been waiting for all year seem to drop at that time. To handle the peaks and valleys in proposal workload, get additional proposal expertise for must-win procurements, or get a fresh view on how to present their solutions, companies reach out to proposal consultants. When you need help from proposal consultants, here are some things you should keep in mind.

Best Informed Wins
Collected Articles of Bob Lohfeld from
Washington Technology (2010 – 2012)

A typical proposal can take a dozen or more people to develop over a 30- to 45-day period. During this high-paced activity, you can supplement your own staff with consultants. Proposal consultants include proposal managers, volume leads (technical, management, past performance, and price), subject matter experts, technical writers, coordinators, graphic artists, editors, and production specialists. Each specializes in a different aspect of the proposal-development process, so before you start looking for proposal consultants, determine what skills you need to augment your proposal team.

Engage the consultant early. Proposal managers should be selected and engaged before RFP release. Working tasks pre-proposal, before RFP release, is one of the best ways to raise your win probability and level the workload that occurs when building a proposal. Though a desktop publisher may not be needed until the last week or two of the proposal, engage them early to get the best ones and allow ample time for them to get up to speed on requirements. If you give consultants a running start at their assignment, you'll end up with a better end product.

Best Informed Wins
Collected Articles of Bob Lohfeld from *Washington Technology* (2010 – 2012)

We consistently misuse the term proposal manager because we call every person who manages a proposal a proposal manager, without regard to their management experience or proposal expertise. We recognize skill levels in other management categories, but unfortunately, when it comes to proposal managers, we don't differentiate their seniority and just call them all proposal managers. Things to look for when selecting your proposal manager are:

1. Management expertise

The size of the deal often drives the level of management expertise needed by the proposal manager. Like task leaders, some proposal managers do a fine job managing a five-person proposal but don't have the management expertise or leadership skills to drive a large, complex proposal for a multi-hundred-million-dollar deal to victory in a highly competitive market.

2. Proposal expertise

It takes more than years of experience to develop expertise in the proposal field. Expertise is gained by working on demanding assignments in highly competitive, complex proposals. Just being member of the team does not qualify someone as a proposal expert. If a proposal manager is leading main-thrust proposals for a major company, then presumably that person is managing proposals at the highest end of the competitive spectrum and would have more proposal expertise than someone who is leading proposals in a smaller business competing in a set-aside market. It's like being an all-star in Little League versus the pros—there is generally a world of difference.

3. Agency experience

There are similarities among most proposals written in the federal market, so while it is nice to have agency experience, it is not essential. Proposal managers tend to be more generalists, but some specialize by market segmentation (e.g., defense or civil agencies) and a few develop expertise in specific agencies after having done multiple proposals for those agencies.

4. Domain experience

It is essential that the proposal manager have some understanding of the contract work to be done. Good predictors of this are an undergraduate or advanced degree in a related field, on-the-job work experience in that industry, or experience gained writing proposals for companies in that field.

5. Professional commitment

A professional commitment to the proposal field is important and separates out those who are really accidental proposal consultants, just filling time between other assignments. A professional commitment is often demonstrated by training in proposal development processes and tools. One of the best commitments is participation in industry organizations such as the Association of Proposal Management Professionals.

Low cost does not prevail. If your company is hiring a consultant, presumably it's because you need someone with real experience and expertise. This is the time to pay for someone who has the qualifications you need to get the job done (and win the proposal). The old adage *You get what you pay for* is never truer than with consultants. Determine exactly how much experience you need, and pay for the person with that experience.

Once you select your proposal consultant, have an expectations-setting meeting as the very first thing you do. It is important to set expectations early in regard to job responsibilities, personalities and working styles, and lines of authority. Clearly communicate the consultant's roles, responsibilities, and reporting relationships to the proposal team. The consultant needs the real authority to set schedules and meetings and obtain resources with the complete and transparent backing of the sponsor.

Don't undermine the consultant by ignoring requests to provide requested resources, facilities, and equipment, and don't set meetings for the proposal team without discussing with the consultant first. Support the consultant in his or her leadership role. With the right consultant and your company's support, everyone should see the proposal moving on a clear path to victory.

WashingtonTechnology.com, August 2, 2010

3 Steps to improving your proposals

Break the cycle of relearning key lessons each time around

No proposal is ever perfect. Every company executive wishes he or she had just a few more days to tweak the last sections. But, after the proposal goes out the door, it is time to reflect on what did or did not go well in the proposal process and what could have been done to improve the outcome. A review of lessons learned is a valuable step in improving proposal development efficiency and raising your win probability on the next bid.

Surprisingly, not all companies do such reviews. Even more surprisingly, many companies that do them repeatedly make the same mistakes. The review should follow the same process after every significant proposal. The process has these three fundamental steps.

1. Gather data

Give the proposal team a few days to settle back into its normal operations before trying to collect information about the last proposal. People need time to reflect—but not so much time that they forget what they learned. One or two weeks is typically the right time frame to begin data collection.

Start the data collection process by selecting the participants and inviting them to join in the review. Participants should include the proposal team, technical and management contributors, executive team, and subcontractors. Congratulate the team on the successful proposal delivery and set expectations for the review. Ask the participants to reflect on the proposal process and their experience on the proposal team. This will enable them to share their perspective on what they could have done differently to improve the process and the proposal.

Designate someone to be the recipient of all the comments and ask each participant to send comments to that person. Ask for comments covering the full life cycle of procurement, not just the proposal development phase. You will want comments about opportunity qualification, pursuit and pre-proposal phases in addition to the proposal development phase. For each phase, each participant should address three fundamental questions: what went well, what didn't go well, and how activities could have been done differently to improve the process and the proposal.

2. Analyze data

Begin by sorting the comments along the procurement timeline. For example, group all comments dealing with pre-proposal activities together and then sort those into subcategories by comment type: what worked well, what didn't and how to improve. Combine redundant or similar comments and edit out comments about an individual's performance or comments that might become career-limiting expressions of personal dissatisfaction. Those are personnel issues to be dealt with separately and are not part of a process improvement review.

Use a three-column table to show the analysis results. The columns are symptoms, root causes, and recommendations. Most comments will describe symptoms, not the root cause of the problem. For example, writers who consistently miss deadlines could be a symptom of several different root causes. Perhaps they are overworked and fully billable during the day, the corporate culture doesn't enforce deadlines, or they never had proposal training. Whatever the reasons, getting at the root cause is critical because treating symptoms just masks the real problems.

This is the hardest part of the analysis because most people treat the symptoms without ever understanding the root cause of the problems. We need to fix what is broken, not just treat the symptoms—and of course, we want to preserve what is working and be open to accepting improvement suggestions.

3. Learn from mistakes

Brief corporate management and the proposal team with the results of the analysis. Give them time to understand the findings and accept the recommendations. Improvement requires careful changes to processes, better training for participants and investments in better technology. Implementing them requires consensus and a road map for change.

Best Informed Wins
Collected Articles of Bob Lohfeld from
Washington Technology **(2010 – 2012)**

If you conduct your lessons learned review correctly and after every proposal, you can break the cycle of relearning the same lessons after each major proposal.

WashingtonTechnology.com, August 27, 2010

What the government won't tell you about your proposal

When you talk, be prepared and know what is left unsaid

Congratulations, your proposal has made competitive range, and the government has contacted you to discuss your offer. What the government will and won't tell you in these discussions can be a surprise to the unprepared bidder, but sophisticated players know the rules and what to expect.

First, it is important to know if your dialogue with the government is a discussion or a clarification. There is a difference, and it is important to which type of communication is being requested.

Best Informed Wins
Collected Articles of Bob Lohfeld from *Washington Technology* (2010 – 2012)

Discussions are a formal part of the federal procurement process that allows the government to engage in a substantive dialogue with offerors. They occur after the competitive range determination.

If you engage in discussions, a meaningful two-way exchange of information, then you are entitled to revise any part of your proposal you desire—unless, of course, the government tells you otherwise.

If you engage in clarifications, responding to requests from the government to clarify what you wrote, then you are not entitled to change your proposal. Always confirm which type of communication is being requested if you're not clear.

Discussions need not be equal

When agencies enter into discussion with offerors, they do not have to treat offerors equally. For example, an agency can have discussions with one offeror about its price proposal and not discuss any other sections of that offeror's proposal. For a second offeror in the competitive range for the same procurement, the agency has no obligation to discuss that offeror's price proposal even though they did with the first. However, when conducting exchanges with offerors, agency personnel may not "engage in conduct that…favors one offeror over another," (Federal Acquisition Regulation (FAR) 15.306(e)(1)); in particular, agencies may not engage in what amounts to disparate treatment of competing offerors.

Discussions need not be comprehensive

The government has no obligation to discuss weaknesses in your proposal, even though you might presume that is the purpose of discussions. FAR 15.306(d)(3)) is skillfully written so that when conducting discussions with offerors in the competitive range, those discussions include "at a minimum…deficiencies, significant weaknesses, and adverse past performance information to which the offeror has not yet had an opportunity to respond."

Agencies are not required to afford offerors all-encompassing discussions or to discuss every aspect of a proposal that receives less than the maximum score. Agencies are not required to advise an offeror of a minor weakness that is not considered significant, even when the weakness subsequently becomes a determinative factor in choosing between two closely ranked proposals.

If the agency determines that your proposal is full of weaknesses that are not deemed significant, it does not need to discuss them.

Discussions are not intended to provide the whole truth about how the agency scored your proposal.

Discussions must be meaningful

When an agency engages in discussions with an offeror, the discussions must be meaningful—sufficiently detailed to lead an offeror into proposal areas requiring amplifications or revisions that materially enhance its potential for receiving the award. The government may help you rid your proposal of significant weaknesses and deficiencies—assuming you made competitive range—but don't expect it to lead you to eliminate weaknesses in your offer.

If you understand the discussion rules, you'll know that discussions focus on remedying significant weaknesses in your proposal, not on leveling the playing field. Be prepared to correct these significant weaknesses—and any other hidden weaknesses when you submit your revised final proposal.

WashingtonTechnology.com, December 14, 2010

3 Keys to creating winning proposals

A defined and efficient process is essential to success

Creating winning proposals is not the same as writing a proposal. Anyone can write a proposal for government work, given enough time and resources. However, only one bidder writes the winning proposal. The best proposals have three things in common:

1. They are directed and written by talented people experienced at writing proposals.
2. They follow a similar, defined process.
3. They are designed in an environment that creates proposals efficiently.

Best Informed Wins
Collected Articles of Bob Lohfeld from
Washington Technology (2010 – 2012)

Your capture and proposal managers bring necessary skills to plan, staff, lead, and control your capture campaign and develop your competitive proposal. They work as a team and understand each member's role. The capture manager leads the campaign, and the proposal manager comes in before a request for proposals is released to focus on developing the proposal.

This team knows that the first step is developing a winning solution. During the capture phase and pre-proposal phases, they work together to:

- **Create a clear win strategy.** Win strategies derive from a competitive assessment that focuses on your competitors' strengths and weaknesses. Understanding these enable you to create a win strategy that highlights your strengths and mitigates your weaknesses while neutralizing your competitors' strengths and accentuating their weaknesses.

- **Develop and document the solution.** Solution development begins during the pursuit phase as a separate exercise from writing the proposal. Create and document your solution, complete design trade-offs, conduct reviews and approve the solution before writing the technical and management response.

- **Build in significant strengths.** Every winning proposal is rich in features that evaluators will assess as proposal strengths. These features are engineered into your proposed solution to show that your approach increases your likelihood of successful performance or that your solution exceeds a requirement in a way that is beneficial to the government customer. Those strengths are explained to the selecting official along with your price and used as the basis to differentiate competitors and justify selection of the winner.

Although each proposal is different, the process used to create winning proposals generally has these characteristics.

- **Early proposal planning and development.** Great proposals begin during the pursuit stage well in advance of the final RFP. Pre-proposal activities are funded, a proposal manager and support staff are assigned, and proposal development begins. Draft text and graphics are created in anticipation of the RFP. That includes the technical description of your solution, management organization structure and management plans, past-performance summaries, key employees' résumés, management and technical processes, and data calls to team members. Portions of significant proposals and any proposal designated as must-win should be substantially written before RFP release.

- **A compliant, easy-to-evaluate proposal structure.** Winning proposals always comply with the RFP. The proposal structure follows RFP instructions and evaluated information is easily found. Good proposal structures are developed early, validated independently, and approved before authors begin writing. The structure must be well crafted because it serves as the foundation for the proposal.

- **Proposal sections designed before writing.** Each section is designed using either an annotated outline technique or a storyboard.

- **Responsive and compelling proposal text.** Text responds completely to the RFP, assertions are substantiated by evidence—not rhetoric—and benefits are clear to the customer. The proposal is written compellingly and is easy to read and score.

Winning proposals are developed in an environment with a well-established proposal development process, using appropriate tools to facilitate the process. A collaborative workspace for archiving capture data and managing proposal development, workflows, and version control is essential. Virtual meeting tools are vital for reviewing documents and hosting discussions. Publishing tools bring efficiency to the process. Up-to-date company databases of past-performance summaries, personnel résumés, prewritten proposal material, proposal graphics, and past proposals are equally helpful.

How do your proposals stack up against these characteristics?

WashingtonTechnology.com, June 14, 2010

10 Reasons why you need capture management

A successful strategy requires buy-in from corporate leaders and a documented process

When we examine why companies win or lose new business in the government market, the reasons are amazingly similar. Companies win more often when they focus on understanding customer requirements and objectives. They predictably lose more often when they don't. Similarly, qualifying new business opportunities early in the business development life cycle results in better win rates, while late qualification results in fewer wins and cost increases in business development.

Best Informed Wins
Collected Articles of Bob Lohfeld from *Washington Technology* (2010 – 2012)

These and other activities are strong indicators of how well a company will do in competitive procurements. This correlation provides clear evidence that companies can raise their win probabilities by performing certain activities well and in the right sequence, thereby establishing the basis for an efficient process known as capture management.

Each company implements its capture management process to fit its culture and management structure, and all implementations should include the same fundamental activities.

- **Qualify the opportunity.** Assess the new business opportunity and make an appropriate decision to invest in the pursuit.

- **Build the capture plan and resource the capture team.** Develop a realistic, achievable plan that can be accomplished within the time available and against which capture progress can be measured.

- **Understand the customer's objectives and requirements.** Take the time to fully understand the customer's scope of work and the objectives to be achieved.

- **Develop a preliminary solution linked to objectives.** Create a solution to perform the work that achieves the customer's objectives.

- **Position with the customer.** Preview your solution with the client to shape the procurement strategy and the client's thinking.

- **Assess the competition.** Build a thorough, competitive assessment on which to base your win strategy and price to win.

- **Develop a win strategy.** Identify your company's strengths and competitors' weaknesses so you can mitigate your weaknesses, neutralize their strengths, and accentuate your positive discriminators.

- **Establish a price to win.** Establish a target price based on your competitive strategy and expected competitor pricing.

- **Plan and execute a teaming strategy.** Identify where teammates can bolster your position, and select the best teaming partners and negotiate teaming agreements.

- **Assess risk.** Identify, analyze, and mitigate contract performance risk as perceived by the customer.

Defining your process is the first step toward implementing capture management. This requires developing detailed procedures that mesh with your company's corporate culture, along with supporting templates to make the process efficient. It takes several iterations to ensure that you establish a defined, repeatable process that works.

Full endorsement and support by corporate leadership and management are critical to capture process success. Some stakeholders are reluctant to establish a prescribed process, arguing that they were successful without it and don't want to change what has worked for them. Winning them over is a cultural transformation challenge that takes the full support of corporate leadership.

Best Informed Wins
Collected Articles of Bob Lohfeld from *Washington Technology* (2010 – 2012)

Over time, you accumulate data from your pursuits and can analyze that data to measure the effectiveness and efficiency of your capture process. Based on that analysis, you can measure results and adjust your processes, providing a quantifiable basis for capture process optimization for your company, culture, and market segmentation.

So why capture management? A defined, repeatable, managed, measured, and optimized approach provides multifaceted benefits. It will:

- Result in winning more business from fewer, better-qualified opportunities.
- Raise overall win probability.
- Decrease costs.
- Improve the quality of life for everyone involved.

Additionally, the process is scalable as your business grows.

Why not? Maybe you think your firm is too small and that defining and implementing a process takes too much time and investment. Maybe there's a sense that everyone is just too busy to stop and think about doing it better. Maybe your firm's heroes think they don't need a process.

There are myriad reasons for or against a capture management process.

WashingtonTechnology.com, April 29, 2010

Best Informed Wins

Collected Articles of Bob Lohfeld from *Washington Technology* (2010 – 2012)

Resolve to improve your win rate

Focus on capture management and associated activities from the decision to pursue through award

Let it be resolved that 2010 will be the year in which we raise our new business win rate, write better proposals that cost us less to create, and leave the practice of working to exhaustion on late-night proposals as our final fond memory from the year now past.

This New Year's resolution will probably be made by executives at half the companies that work in the highly competitive government technology market. Yet few companies will change how they pursue new business, prepare for proposals, or handle the demanding task of writing proposals when the request for proposals arrives.

To help achieve this New Year's resolution, let's focus on capture management and what companies should do from the time they decide to pursue a new opportunity until the award is made.

Along with examining the capture management process, we will explore each of its activities. Capture management is a defined, repeatable, managed, measured, and optimized methodology used by successful companies in the government market to win new business.

For new entrants in the government market, their capture management process is probably still undefined, and the pursuit of every new business opportunity looks like a new adventure. Entrepreneurs will soon learn that successful pursuits follow a similar path, and from that path, a process is born. It is then tried on the next several pursuits and modified until it fits the management style and the dynamics of the market the company serves. This process is then declared to be defined and repeatable.

Best Informed Wins
Collected Articles of Bob Lohfeld from
Washington Technology (2010 – 2012)

Management begins to see its value and embraces it as the path for continued success. All new business pursuits are managed through the process, and any exceptions are discouraged. Management follows the process as prescribed, reinforcing its use across the enterprise.

Capture management infrastructure begins to emerge as the repository for data for all capture activities. This repository, with its templates and information reused from previous successful pursuits, further crystallizes capture management as one of the key features of the company's success. With good data and lessons learned from successful pursuits, the effectiveness and efficiency of the capture process is measured and adjusted to make incremental improvements. As each improvement is made, the process becomes better optimized for the company's type of business, market, and competitive environment.

Whether you are new to the government market or one of the Top 100, you will continually work your capture process to improve your win probability, reduce your new business acquisition costs, and improve the quality of life for all those involved.

Best Informed Wins
Collected Articles of Bob Lohfeld from *Washington Technology* **(2010 – 2012)**

In the coming months, we'll take a close look at this process and capture activities such as understanding customer requirements and objectives, positioning to win, creating winning proposals, interpreting evaluation criteria, managing the capture and proposal process, and using lessons learned to improve your win probability.

Until next month, let us loudly proclaim our New Year's resolution—and when asked how we are going to do that, tell everyone the details will follow.

WashingtonTechnology.com, January 27, 2010

Best Informed Wins
Collected Articles of Bob Lohfeld from
Washington Technology (2010 – 2012)

Ask the right questions to understand customer objectives

How well do you understand your customer's requirements and objectives?

Did you know the leading indicator for predicting whether you will be successful in a government bid is how well you understand the customer's requirements and objectives?

As a capture team leader, one of your first jobs is to understand and document your customer's requirements and objectives. Requirements are the activities a company must do when it performs the contract. They

Best Informed Wins
Collected Articles of Bob Lohfeld from *Washington Technology* (2010 – 2012)

include technical and management tasks described in the scope of work, generally found in section C of a federal government request for proposals. But, they can also reside in other sections and attachments to the RFP.

On the other hand, objectives are more elusive. They are the desired outcomes that the government hopes to achieve by having a company perform the contract requirements in an exceptional manner. Every bidder will offer to perform the contract requirements, but the successful bidder will show how its approach ensures the government's objectives are achieved. It is not sufficient simply to offer to perform the contract requirements—you must propose to perform them in a way that makes your customer's program a success.

RFPs generally do not contain objectives and must be deduced from research or discussions with government personnel—preferably before the RFP is released. Because those discussions are so important, you must plan and practice so you know what questions you are going to ask and who is going to ask them.

To ensure capture teams ask the right questions, consider running a practice exercise in which all team members write 10 questions they would like to have answered when meeting with the government. Gather those questions, and divide them into three categories. The first category comprises questions about requirements. The second includes questions about objectives. The third includes questions that might not be appropriate to ask because the customer might be reluctant to answer.

Next, within each category, eliminate duplicate questions and consolidate similar questions. Order the questions from the best to worst based on how important the prospective answer is to the team. Finally, word the questions to ensure that each is clear and asked in a way that gives a high likelihood of returning an answer with the insight need.

Divide the final questions among team members who will attend the meeting with the government. If possible, conduct a mock government meeting with the capture team coach acting as the government executive. All participants ask their assigned question as they would at the meeting. This exercise lets participants practice the questions and helps the team decide the order in which to ask questions. Generally, the team begins with questions about requirements and then moves to questions about objectives. After several practice sessions, the team is armed with well-crafted questions presented in a logical and insightful manner, and it is ready for the real meeting.

This exercise yields multiple benefits. The capture team will ask important and relevant questions during its meeting, which will yield answers for a good understanding of both government's requirements and objectives. The government benefits from a well-structured, efficient meeting with a meaningful exchange of questions and answers. The interchange demonstrates that your company understands this business, is highly professional, and is the kind of contractor the government wants.

Understanding customer requirements is one of the first steps in capture management and is fundamental to winning. The better you understand these requirements and objectives, the higher your win probability. As capture manager and coach, your mantra is simple: The best informed wins.

WashingtonTechnology.com, April 5, 2010

5 Passing grades you need to lead the pack

Preview solutions with government stakeholders to validate assumptions and build advocacy for your offering

Ever wonder why some companies appear to be the odds-on favorite to win a contract?

A well-orchestrated, pre-request for proposals ritual goes on long before a procurement is released for bid. Company business development, technical and management professionals step up the frequency of visits to their customers to better understand customer objectives and to perfect their company's solution. Those professionals also preview their solutions with government stakeholders to validate assumptions and build advocacy for their company's offering.

Best Informed Wins
Collected Articles of Bob Lohfeld from *Washington Technology* (2010 – 2012)

Their focus is simple: ensuring their proposed solution meets or exceeds government requirements and resonates with the customer

Those industry professionals work to shape the agency's procurement strategy, ensuring it is favorable to their firm and the solutions they will propose. Offering insights on procurement strategy; choice of contract vehicles; RFP instructions, evaluation factors, subfactors, and criteria; contract terms and conditions; and pricing approaches are the norm. Discussion topics in some procurements, such as the Air Force tanker contract, include single award versus multiple award. Other pursuits focus on full-and-open competition versus set-aside programs and which of the many set-aside types should be used. Should the government limit proposals to 50 pages or 500 pages? Should there be two or 20 key personnel résumés? Should the award be made on the basis of best value or does the technically acceptable lowest price win? All are important considerations, and the top contenders will have a voice in the outcome of each.

Throughout this positioning ritual, companies aim to be viewed by the customer as one of the small group of top contenders for award.

Best Informed Wins
Collected Articles of Bob Lohfeld from
Washington Technology (2010 – 2012)

Positioning Effectiveness Score Card

Positioning Objective	Assessment Criteria
Understand requirements and objectives	Requirements and objectives discussed with multiple people at customer organization
Establish company credibility and interest	Company viewed as a leader with known corporate, technical and project management teams in addition to solid past performance and experience
Preview preliminary solution with customer	Well-developed solution with features linked to objectives and approach vetted with customer to get buy-in and solution validation
Achieve acceptance of win strategy (technical, management, past performance, teaming, price) accepted by customer	Win strategy well established, previewed, and accepted by customer
Influence the RFP	Procurement strategy, proposal instructions, and evaluation criteria favorable

Positioning is important

Positioning is one of the fundamental steps in capture management. As a capture manager, you want to ensure the government knows your firm and its reputation for excellence, in addition to your management team, planned technical approach, past performance and ability to price competitively. You want to validate your understanding of the government's requirements and objectives, test the features of your solution to ensure that they bring value to the customer, and present your teaming strategy and team members. Finally, you want to validate that your win strategy separates your firm from other top contenders.

A positioning score card is a useful tool to assess how well you are positioned. The sidebar figure shows a typical score card used to measure the effectiveness of your positioning campaign. It describes each positioning objective and the criteria used to assess how well you achieved each objective. Additional objectives, such as risk, past performance, teaming and so on, can be added based on your specific circumstances and the competitive field. If you cannot show that you have accomplished each positioning objective, you have work to do. If you run out of time to do the required positioning work, it is likely that others are better positioned in this race.

Your goal should be to position your firm as the top contender. Proper positioning lays the groundwork for a win well before the acquisition takes place and makes you a partner in the acquisition development. If you help define the battlefield, your odds of winning increase.

WashingtonTechnology.com, March 3, 2010

3 Critical steps to surviving tough times

People, training, and technology are critical

There's little doubt that the federal budget will undergo some contractions this year, either because Congress will reduce spending levels outright for some agencies or the inevitable flow of continuing resolutions will postpone approval for new spending levels. As budgets shrink, there will be fewer new contracts in the government contractor market. With fewer deals to compete for, contractors will need to raise their level of competitiveness to win their share.

Now is the time to invest in new business acquisition, not scale back. Companies making investments in people, processes and technology will raise their level of competitiveness and, in the face of a tightening market, will win their share of new business. Companies failing to meet these new challenges will become casualties as they watch the market change and competitions become more demanding.

Invest in people

You can raise the level of competitiveness of your business development (BD), capture management and proposal development team in several ways.

First, select the right professionals. You want people who deeply understand your business and your market and can compete at the intellectual level demanded by this heightened competition. This is your core business acquisition team and can be augmented by consultants who specialize in the government market.

Next, provide basic and advanced training to improve their skills and increase their effectiveness. Training in BD, capture management, proposal management, and proposal writing are important steps in maintaining and improving professional skills.

Whether you choose internal or external training programs, instruction should be designed and delivered by training specialists who are experts in the government market.

Finally, coach your team to perform at the highest levels of competitiveness. Coaching must be delivered by highly skilled professionals who know how to compete and win at this new level of play. If you do not have these coaching resources on staff, look to consultants to augment your team.

Improve business acquisition processes

As competition increases, business processes become more important for competing at higher levels. Your business acquisition processes should be well defined, repeatable, managed, measured, and optimized for the market you serve. Processes should be integrated from new business opportunity identification through the capture, pre-proposal, and proposal phases—and even integrated with contract performance.

Quality reviews should be built into the process at appropriate intervals and used to raise your level of competitiveness. Standard procedures with data collection templates should be used for all steps in the process. Those increase process efficiency and improve the completeness and quality of information.

Archive documents in an enterprise repository to ensure availability to all authorized participants. Lessons learned from each pursuit should be archived in this repository, and process performance metrics should be collected and analyzed to provide a quantitative basis for process improvement and optimization.

Use technology

Technology has become an essential enabler for the modern BD organization. Pipeline management tools track the progress of new opportunities across the acquisition life cycle. Workflow management tools aide in automating capture and proposal processes. Collaborative virtual workspaces are routinely used to manage capture and proposal activities. Those tools seamlessly integrate employees and team members into the new business acquisition process.

Enterprise repositories should house documents such as marketing plans, capture plans, bid strategies, design documents, current and past proposals, graphics libraries, company résumés, and past-performance contract references. Virtual tools are used to conduct sales, capture and proposal discussions versus traveling to face-to-face meetings.

The path forward

Those who invest in business acquisition should see payoffs in increased win rates, improved efficiency, and more new business revenue. Those who don't will likely lag behind the leaders, merge with other firms or cede parts of their business portfolio to others in the market. Which path you choose is the most important choice you can make in a shrinking market.

WashingtonTechnology.com, April 4, 2011

Pitfalls to avoid in a down market

Avoid chasing too many opportunities and rushing headlong into new markets

With all the talk about budget cuts, we see some companies overreacting and altering their bidding strategies. Budget reduction numbers out of Congress indicate that 2011 spending will decline by $38 billion.

According to Ray Bjorklund, senior vice president and chief knowledge officer at FedSources, the challenge is determining how many of those dollars are attached to contracts. "There's spending, and there's contract spending," Bjorklund said. "A significant amount of the $38 billion is in government compensation loan programs, and subsidies and therefore not contractor-addressable."

The net authority that agencies have to spend on compensation and contracts—but not loans, grants or subsidies—in fiscal 2011 is $1.8 trillion, and it is this amount that was hit by the $38 billion in cuts. Although $38 billion is a large amount, it represents only 2% of the total spending authority.

Meanwhile, reactive, quick-fix strategy changes can often be detrimental to a company for a few reasons.

Bid-everything strategy

The shortsighted approach of increasing the operational tempo of the proposal department without increasing other investments often reduces new business revenues. I heard one sales executive say, "To make our sales number, we have to bid more deals—so we are going to bid everything."

Although this strategy certainly increases the number and value of deals in the new business pipeline, without actively working to qualify those deals, that is often just a cosmetic fix and does not mean new business revenues will follow.

Best Informed Wins
Collected Articles of Bob Lohfeld from *Washington Technology* (2010 – 2012)

The bid-everything strategy falls short because to bid more, a company might end up lowering or even abandoning its bid-qualification standards and business-acquisition processes. Bidding more jobs does not mean winning more jobs. Winning is a complex undertaking that requires robust deal qualification standards, investments in executing well-planned capture programs, and talented people to write compliant, responsive, compelling and feature-rich proposals.

Working harder doesn't mean working smarter. Just churning out more proposals will not necessarily increase revenues. In fact, the results are often predictable. Bidding more deals often results in a company bidding on opportunities that it is unqualified for or unprepared to bid. That forces employees to work harder in a desperate attempt to win. Win rates decline, and good employees leave the company in search of a more reasonable work environment.

New market strategy

Shifting business development efforts to new markets and temporarily suspending business development in the company's core business areas is another over-correction strategy.

Although that can be a preservation move if your core market is disappearing, it is shortsighted if it as an overreaction to market dynamics. Exploring new markets and entering new markets are two different things. It is easy to send everyone to explore new markets, but successfully winning business in new markets takes a well-planned campaign—and it takes time.

Most companies explore new markets, bid a few deals with predictable results, quickly lose interest, and return to their core markets while lamenting the distraction from core business to explore and chase frivolous opportunities.

Focus and invest strategy

Staying focused on your core markets and increasing investment in new business acquisition is a better strategy in a downturn market. This requires investment across the full acquisition life cycle. That means increasing opportunity identification, capture management, pre-proposal preparation, and proposal development efforts—and investing in people, processes, and technology.

Improving your staff's business acquisition skill sets is the best investment you can make, and company-provided training is an excellent way to develop those skills. Improved processes for business development, capture management, and proposal development can increase win rates and decrease costs. Technology investments can increase efficiency and effectiveness. All those activities collaborate to create a focused strategy that will increase new business.

Remember, in a contracting market, competition levels will increase, and the strongest will survive and prosper. If your game plan is sound, stay focused, invest, and do not become distracted.

WashingtonTechnology.com, April 25, 2011

Why your win rate is hurting your business

If you win every bid, you might be too conservative

Win rates vary widely among companies, and we see them range from as low as 10% to as high as 80% based on a variety of factors, including companies that bid anything and everything to those that bid too conservatively. To assess how your win rate stacks up against your competition, take a look below. Equally important, examine the details behind your win rate. These can direct you to areas where you can make substantive improvements.

Win rate: 80% to 100%
Color score: Green

Assessment and recommendations for improvement: Doing very well, but opportunity qualification and bid decision criteria are set too conservatively. Adjust these criteria slightly to increase the number of procurements you bid, and you will significantly increase new business revenue.

Win rate: 50% to 79%
Color score: Blue

Assessment and recommendations for improvement: You are in the zone. Your capture and proposal processes are working, people are trained in effective capture and proposal management—as well as writing—and you are using technology to increase business acquisition efficiency. Focus on optimizing your capture and proposal process and driving greater efficiency into your business development life cycle.

Win rate: 25% to 49%
Color score: Green

Assessment and recommendations for improvement: Not bad, but you could certainly do better. Focus on defining and institutionalizing capture and proposal processes. Invest in infrastructure to increase business acquisition efficiency. Work on improving people skills by emphasizing training in capture and proposal management and in proposal writing.

Win rate: 0 to 24%
Color score: Red

Assessment and recommendations for improvement: You're in trouble and need to rethink everything you're doing. You are bidding jobs you have no business bidding, and your processes—if you have them—are broken. It is back to basics. Define your capture and proposal processes, set pursuit and bid criteria, and train your staff in capture and proposal management and in proposal writing. Create an enterprise repository to manage your business acquisition activities. You have much room for improvement.

As a rule, you can look at win rates to gauge the overall effectiveness of your business acquisition process. We like to see win rates in the 50 to 75% range. Larger companies with mature processes and well-trained capture and proposal managers consistently deliver results in this range.

If your win rates fall to the bottom of the win rate scale, it's time to rethink everything. Go back to basics and define your capture and proposal processes. Manage to these processes, and train your staff in the roles they have to perform. Make sure you have suitable automation to support your processes, and make sure everyone follows the processes. Every company with good processes and supportive infrastructure should deliver win rates above 25%.

Occasionally, we see win rates that are too high. Generally, this occurs when a company is bidding too conservatively, e.g., they are working in a narrowly defined market niche and don't venture out of their comfort zone. If the company opens up its bid criteria slightly and takes on more bidding risk, it can greatly increase its revenue.

Computing win rates

We define win rate as the number of competitive proposals you win in a given period divided by the number of competitive proposals you submit. Don't include any proposals where the government canceled the procurement since these events are generally outside your control.

Don't create win rates based on dollars won versus dollars bid. This simply distorts your win rate. When companies do this, you can bet they have a poor underlying win rate and are hiding that by counting the values of some large indefinite-delivery, indefinite-quantity contract to inflate their numbers. The number you want is wins divided by total proposals submitted.

To compute a statistically valid win rate, you must have competed more than a few times. While it is mathematically correct to say, "If you submit two proposals and win one, you have a win rate of 50%," it is hardly accurate to say that you are likely to continue winning 50% of all proposals you submit. Basically, the more competitive proposals you submit, the more statistically valid your win rate.

Looking behind the numbers

To understand how well your company is performing, compute your win rate by type of procurement. For example, if you bid both 8(a) procurements and full-and-open procurements, compute separate win rates for each. You may be surprised to find that while you do well on 8(a) competitions, your win rate on full-and-open procurements is in the cellar. Clearly, you must do more work on your people, processes, and infrastructure to bid full-and-open competitions effectively.

Similarly, examine win rates on competitive task-order contracts. These can reveal problems in handling rapid-response procurements.

Finally, look at win rates by procurement dollar value. We often see companies that do well bidding smaller procurements but whose win rates tank when contract values go above $30 million.

A good analysis of win rates should show you where you fall short and where to focus efforts to improve your company's revenue growth.

WashingtonTechnology.com, May 24, 2011

5 Predictions for the 2020 Market

Will things be better or worse or both?

Capture and proposal management, as a practice and a profession, continually changes. Recently, we asked leading professionals what changes they expect to see by 2020, and I think some of the predictions will surprise you. Here are some humorous as well as common-sense extensions of where we are today and what you might expect to see in coming years.

Government market

The government push to insource will have disappeared, having been debated and resolved at least once in each of the last three decades. Government and industry will be partners, working together to streamline acquisition processes and reduce wasteful proposal requirements (and time spent on the activity). Government procurement organizations will have been substantially rebuilt. The need for hard-copy proposal submissions will have disappeared or diminished sharply, especially with the push for green computing. I think sophisticated multimedia proposals versus text-heavy submissions will increase companies' competitive positioning (remember the videotape submissions of the 1990s.)

As socio-economic legislation runs its course, the emphasis will shift from the government helping small businesses to large businesses doing this via mentor-protégé relationships sanctioned by government agencies. Performance-based contracting will finally be understood by both government and industry and be increasing significantly, so the need for quality certifications and processes for contractors to meet service-level agreements and performance standards will be on the upswing.

Workforce

The workforce will be more diverse based on population shifts away from cities, and

Best Informed Wins
Collected Articles of Bob Lohfeld from *Washington Technology* (2010 – 2012)

professionals will be employed in a virtual world without regard to where they reside. Baby boomers will be in their 70s and still actively engaged in the workforce either on a part- or full-time basis. New entrants into the workforce at the end of the decade are only 10 years old today. They have never seen a world without the Internet, expect the world to stream to them at light speed wherever they are, and have significant experience using collaborative software to complete projects.

Employees will work on global government projects where work is performed in virtual space and staffed by people from multiple countries brought together for their technical expertise, without regard to cultural or geopolitical backgrounds.

The workforce will be able to support the entire bid life cycle, instead of discrete segments such as proposals or capture. Technology proficiency will be mandatory, and those who are slow to adopt or resist technology entirely will face dwindling prospects.

Business development, capture management, and proposal management will be a recognized, accredited profession with 15,000 people holding accreditations, and the Association for Proposal Management Professionals (APMP) will be the leading accrediting organization. BD, capture, and proposal professionals will hold multiple accreditations and certifications from leading professional associations, consulting firms, colleges, and universities. Professional development training in these areas will be the norm, not the exception.

Process

There will be a strong connection between technology and workflow to enforce process rigor and increase efficiency. BD, capture management, and proposal development processes will become more agile and refined to fit shorter procurement life cycles. We will place renewed emphasis on process maturity. Process optimization will be based on actual measurements taken across multiple capture and proposal efforts and will use statistical analysis as the basis for process change. Companies will implement BD, capture management, and proposal development into an integrated workflow management system that serves as the corporate repository to manage all new business pursuits.

Best Informed Wins
Collected Articles of Bob Lohfeld from *Washington Technology* (2010 – 2012)

Technology

Virtual businesses will avoid brick-and-mortar costs, reducing operations costs and increasing their competitive edge. Mainstream companies will exist in virtual space with no physical offices. Cloud computing will be accepted as the norm, IT security protection will be expected, and IT infrastructure will be designed for virtual workforces. Both contractor and government workforces will telecommute, and geographic boundaries will diminish as virtual meetings replace trips to personal offices.

Transportation

While computing will be ubiquitous, we will still be plagued with transportation problems. Traffic will become so congested around major cities that employers will always offer alternative work schedules and telework options. The Washington Beltway will regularly come to a standstill and no longer be considered a reliable transportation corridor. The Tysons Corner area will be in its eighth year of modernizing, and Maryland will be in its 40th year of studying the environmental impact of building an outer beltway. The Silver Line will finally reach Dulles Airport.

As strategic planners, we build our plans for the world we will live in in the future—not the one we share today. I hope these insights help you better plan for your future in capture and proposal management.

WashingtonTechnology.com, July 7, 2011

Best Informed Wins
Collected Articles of Bob Lohfeld from *Washington Technology* **(2010 – 2012)**

7 tips for crafting a dominant proposal summary

Focus on the customer, be feature rich, and help evaluators maximize your score

Not all requests for proposals (RFP) call for an Executive Summary, and when proposals must have limited pages, it might be best to skip an Executive Summary.

But, for large proposals or RFPs that ask for an Executive Summary, here are seven steps to creating an effective one.

1. Decide when to write

I'm in the camp that believes later is better. An Executive Summary is a summary of your proposal, and if you haven't written the proposal, it is hard to write an effective summary. If you decide to write your Executive Summary early to give guidance to your proposal team about your approach and major strengths, plan to write twice.

2. Stay focused

An effective Executive Summary provides an overview of your proposal and highlights the features that will be scored as strengths in the evaluation. Clearly tie the features of your approach to the benefits the client will receive. An Executive Summary is about what you propose to do and how you are going to do it. Writing about how great your company is what you do in sales brochures, not in executive summaries.

3. Follow your proposal

Your Executive Summary is a digest of your proposal, without all the details. If written correctly, it gives a good overview of your approach, experience, and value. The structure of your Executive Summary should follow the structure of your proposal. Assuming you organized your proposal in accordance with the proposal instructions found in Section L for federal RFPs, your Executive Summary should follow the same outline, unless there are other instructions in the RFP.

4. How to start your Executive Summary

Every Executive Summary should have an opening statement. This is your vision statement that tells the government what you are going to achieve and how you'll deal with its issues/motivators. Think of it as your campaign promise—if you are elected, this is what you are going to accomplish. If the evaluators buy your vision, they are likely to score your proposal favorably. But, if you open your Executive Summary by telling them how great your company is—ignoring the buyer's mission—you will probably lose the evaluator's interest.

5. Content is king

Each section should provide an overview of a piece of your proposal and highlight the features you believe will be scored as strengths. Your Executive Summary tells readers all the features of your proposal that they would discover if they read the entire proposal. The strengths in each section of the Executive Summary should come directly from the body of your proposal and can be pulled from feature/benefit figures at the beginning of each proposal section or the introductory text that begins each section. This way, the Executive Summary pulls the proposal together and tells the evaluator what to look for in each section.

6. Final content check

Ensure that you review the proposal evaluation criteria and include in your Executive Summary everything you want to say that relates to maximizing your point score. Everything in the Executive Summary must be fully explained in the body of the proposal. This is not the place to introduce last-minute ideas that you wish you had time to add to your proposal.

7. Write persuasively

Now that you know how you are going to organize the Executive Summary and the content to be discussed, use the appropriate balance of good graphics and prose to convey your message convincingly.

If you structure your Executive Summary using these seven steps, it will be focused on the customer, be feature rich, and will help the evaluators maximize your proposal score.

WashingtonTechnology.com, August 26, 2011

6 Ways your proposals fail

And what you can do about it

I received a call from a mid-sized *large* business that had submitted a proposal for IT services and had just learned their proposal did not make competitive range. They were irate and wanted to protest, alleging that the government had not fairly evaluated their proposal.

They had hired a proposal consultant, spent lots of money developing their proposal, and were assured their proposal was professionally done. Before filing the protest, the company asked me to review their proposal. Here's what I found when I did the review and what I told them.

Best Informed Wins
Collected Articles of Bob Lohfeld from *Washington Technology* (2010 – 2012)

Professionally developed proposals always have the same characteristics—they are compliant, responsive, compelling, and customer focused. They present a solution that is easy to evaluate and score well—and they are aesthetically attractive. I used each of these criteria while reviewing this company's submission.

Compliant

The proposal's structure is expected to follow the request for proposals (RFP) instructions (section L of this RFP) and also track with the evaluation criteria (section M).

Initially, this proposal followed section L, but then it departed and added sections not called for in sections L or M. It then skipped required section L topics. Finally, some evaluation criteria were never addressed in the proposal. The easiest way to lose points during an evaluation is to not follow the instructions or not address the evaluation criteria. Simply put, this proposal was non-compliant.

Responsive

The content of each proposal section must respond precisely to each topic prescribed in the RFP. The section headings should track to the RFP instructions, and the associated discussions should be consistent with the section headings. When proposal text fails to address the section's heading, the section is non sequitur, e.g., an applicable response does not follow a particular section title.

The proposal seemed to have section text that was lifted from other proposals and pasted into this proposal. The responses were close, but not close enough. To the non-practitioner, much proposal text sounds alike. After all, if the RFP asks for a QA Plan and we give them a Configuration Management Plan, who would know the difference? This proposal team did just that. I scored some of the sections a zero because they failed the responsiveness test.

Compelling

This is a proposal term that describes how convincing or persuasive the proposal is. In government procurements, we expect the proposal to meet the solicitation requirements fully and exceed those requirements, where practical, in a way that is beneficial to the customer. There should be many features in the proposal that demonstrate a high likelihood of contract success or that exceed solicitation requirements. Assertions about company performance and claims about solution features should be substantiated by real evidence, not boastful rhetoric. Features with relevant and substantiated benefits, presented persuasively, provide the basis for selecting one bidder's proposal over another.

In this proposal, as I read through 200 pages of hum drum technical prose, I found features were few and benefits were even fewer. There was no basis for differentiation and no compelling basis for selection. This was not the way to write a proposal.

Customer-focused

Proposals are customer focused, and marketing brochures are company focused. A customer-focused proposal discusses how your company proposes to do the work and the benefits the customer will receive from your performance. If the proposal just brags about how good the company is and how outstanding its processes are, then the proposal is company-focused at best. Company-focused proposals cause evaluators to lose interest, whereas customer-focused proposals hold evaluators' interest and score higher.

Best Informed Wins
Collected Articles of Bob Lohfeld from *Washington Technology* (2010 – 2012)

Slogging through 200 pages about how good this company is does not substitute for a cogent explanation of what the company planned to do and how it was going do it. If I had read one more time that their processes were *best of breed* or *world class*, I think I would have just closed the book and quit reading.

Easy to evaluate

Evaluators generally start their review with the proposal evaluation criteria in section M of the RFP. They build an evaluation checklist, and then go looking through the proposal to find information that addresses the topics in the evaluation checklist. They search for only what they need to find to evaluate the proposal and write up their evaluation results. Call-out boxes, pull quotes, feature/benefit tables, sections headings, and other techniques help draw the evaluator's attention to the appropriate information. Every evaluator will tell you that if they can't find it, they can't score it. Professional proposals are structured so the key evaluation points are extremely easy to find and evaluate.

As you might expect, in this proposal, key evaluations points were missing or not readily found.

Appearance

Proposals should be attractive and easy to read. They should have a consistent document style, appropriate color pallet, paragraph labeling and numbering scheme traceable to the RFP, and an appropriate mix of text and supporting graphics. Single-column text is fine with half-page or quarter-page-size graphics positioned consistently on the page. Graphics should convey the intended message with the appropriate level of detail.

The proposal was attractive, and if you didn't read the content, it looked like it would score pretty well. I gave them high marks for attractiveness and accolades to the desktop publishing team.

At the end of my review, I told the company executives to save their protest money. In this case, the government did them a favor by eliminating their proposal from the competitive range. This proposal was not professionally done, even though they thought it was, and it had no chance of winning. After the review, they agreed not to protest and resolved to do better next time.

WashingtonTechnology.com, October 5, 2011

Best Informed Wins
Collected Articles of Bob Lohfeld from
Washington Technology (2010 – 2012)

How bad are your proposals?

Only 15% of companies said their proposals were always compliant, responsive, and compelling

In last month's column, *6 ways your proposal can fail,* I wrote about a company that submitted a less-than-professional proposal and wondered how pervasive this problem really is. After all, as professional proposal managers, how bad can our proposals really be?

All professional proposal managers strive to make every proposal compliant, responsive, and compelling, yet a recent presentation reinforced my assessment that only about 15% of the firms bidding on U.S. government contracts consistently achieve these fundamental objectives.

Best Informed Wins
Collected Articles of Bob Lohfeld from *Washington Technology* (2010 – 2012)

In a GovCon Business Development Weekly webinar hosted by Deltek's Michael Hackmer, I discussed four fundamentals for creating a winning proposal. The first three fundamentals comprise creating a compliant, responsive, and compelling proposal. We polled the 150 webinar participants from a cross-section of small to large government contractors and asked them to rate how well their proposals did in achieving those three objectives.

What we learned was surprising. Only 15% said their proposals were always compliant, responsive, and compelling. That leave 85% saying their proposals fell short of these primary objectives.

A deeper look at the results showed that only one third said their proposals were generally compliant, responsive, and compelling. That still left about half the respondents saying their proposals generally failed to meet these objectives.

This is certainly cause for concern since we all know that the best way to lose evaluation points immediately is to submit a proposal that is not compliant, responsive, or compelling. What's so troubling about these statistics is that these firms may have proposed wonderful solutions or service offerings, but because of the quality of their proposals, they likely didn't win.

The fourth objective for creating winning proposals is developing a well-defined solution or service offering that is rich in features that deliver real benefits to the customer—and most importantly, developing the solution and features before starting to write the proposal. In the software business, this is analogous to saying, "Let's design before we start coding."

Having a good solution or a well-defined service offering is a prerequisite to writing a good proposal, yet in my experience many companies start writing before actually defining their solution or service offering. The webinar survey data supports my observations about solution-first writing. About one third of respondents do no solution development before writing. They just start writing and hope that a solution emerges. Clearly, these companies have work to do to improve their basic capture and proposal development processes.

The final question we asked was about the use of capture and proposal processes. Good proposals are the result of well-defined capture and proposal processes. Good processes will consistently produce better proposals, improve win rates, and reduce proposal development costs—yet only half the respondents said they had defined capture and proposal processes.

No wonder so many companies' proposals fail. Having little or no process, writing before developing a solution, and failing to meet the compliant, compelling, and responsive standards is a sure way to lose.

I probably should have asked one more question, "How many respondents want to improve their proposal win rate?" But, I guess the answer is obvious since that's why they participated in the first place.

View webinar presentation and audience Q&A session referenced in this article.

WashingtonTechnology.com, November 14, 2011

How to raise your win rate by 20%

Knowing which investments to make and predicting the payoff is the challenge

All executives want to increase their win rate. If you could raise your company's overall win rate by 20%, the payoff in additional revenue, earnings, and shareholder value could be huge. Company revenues would increase, earnings would increase by the marginal profit rate on the new revenue, and shareholder value would increase proportionally to your increase in earnings.

But, knowing which investments to make and predicting the payoff is the challenge. Here's how to choose your investments and predict the resulting increase in *win rates*.

First, let me make sure everyone understands that we are talking about the investment you make to improve your company's *overall* win rate. This is the average win rate on *all* proposals your company submits, not your win rate on a *specific* proposal. (We use a different model to predict the outcome for individual bids.)

7-Factor Model

To predict increases in overall company win rates, we use a 7-Factor model. Since we are not aware of any other models that do this, we've called it the *Lohfeld 7-Factor Company Win Rate Model*.

While the model predicts overall company win rates, more importantly, it also predicts how a company's win rate is affected by changing investments in these 7 factors—and that's what we're after. If we can predict how the win rate is affected by changes in the 7-Factor score, then we can make investments with confidence, knowing that we can predict the resulting win-rate increase.

The 7-Factor score is based on:

1. **People**. The skills and experience of the people involved in creating proposals.

2. **Business acquisition process**. Business acquisition maturity covering the five stages of business acquisition life cycle.

3. **Tools**. Proposal infrastructure and personal and productivity tools.

4. **Management decision-making**. Qualification and bid decisions.

5. **Solution competitiveness**. Competitive solution with good features and customer benefits.

6. **Proposal quality**. Quality proposals that are always compliant, responsive, and compelling.

7. **Winning culture**. Winning culture with good work/life balance.

We assess each of the factors using four yes/no questions. Each *yes* answer contributes one point to a company's overall score. A perfect assessment scores 28 points and, by the way,

Best Informed Wins
Collected Articles of Bob Lohfeld from *Washington Technology* (2010 – 2012)

we have never seen a company earn all 28 points. Each question takes 15 seconds to read and answer. With 7 factors and 28 questions, it takes 7 minutes to complete the assessment to see how your company rates in each factor.

Here's an example of how the assessment works. The first assessment factor is *People*. Skilled people write better proposals than those who are not so good at it. To assess the skill and experience of the people working capture and proposals, we ask four questions. The answers are based on the skill and experience of your internal staff as well as consultants you use.

The first question is, "Does your capture and proposal core team include your best and brightest professionals, and do they know how to create winning proposals?" You get one point if your answer is *yes* and zero points if the answer is *no*. You get a second point if you answer *yes* to the question, "Are your Proposal Managers always well matched to their assignments and do they always have the right leadership qualities and experience level for the assignment," (or if you don't have the right person available from your in-house team, you go outside your company for proposal management support). You get a third point if you have a career development plan for your proposal professionals, which includes professional development and skills training. You get a fourth point if you can readily add additional proposal resources to augment your team to accommodate fluctuating workloads.

Answer each of these questions with a *yes* or *no*. Each *yes* gets one point, and each *no* gets zero points. If your answer is somewhere between *yes* and *no*, give yourself a half point. Once you complete your 7-Factor Assessment score, you're ready to begin looking at investments.

Selecting investments to raise your win rates

Your strategy is to make company investments that will raise your 7-Factor Assessment score. The higher your assessment score, the higher your overall win rate will be.

Best Informed Wins
Collected Articles of Bob Lohfeld from *Washington Technology* (2010 – 2012)

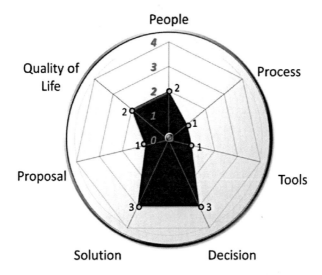

To see which factors to improve, plot your scores on our Lohfeld 7-Axis Diagram. The Lohfeld 7-Axis Diagram provides a graphical representation of your assessment scores and shows at a glance those factors that need to be increased via investments. Invest in factors with the lowest scores first since generally they have a greater variety of investments that will raise your score. Make the least costly investments first with the objective of investing the least amount of money to get the highest increase in scores.

Let's assume that a company wants to make investments to raise the *People* factor. If the scorers went back to their assessment scores, they might find that one of the contributing factors to the low score was that they didn't have a professional development training program for their capture and proposal staff.

Since the company can implement such a program inexpensively, this should be their first planned investment. Similarly, they would use their assessment scores in the *Process* and *Tools* factors to guide them in selecting appropriate investments to raise their scores for these factors.

Using this approach, the company would build a plan of investments to raise its 7-Factor scores systematically and thereby raise its win rates.

Calibrating the model

To measure how much a company's win rate increases with increases in 7-Factor scores, we worked with the Association of Proposal Management Professionals (APMP) and had 45 proposal managers assess their companies and correlate their assessment scores with win rates. We did this exercise at the APMP Nor'easters Chapter Fall Symposium 2011 and the APMP Southern Proposal Accents

Conference (SPAC). Our survey results solidly confirm that companies with higher 7-Factor Assessment scores had higher win rates.

From the APMP data, we found that government contractors with a 20% increase in their 7-Factor Assessment score on average yielded a 20% increase in their win rate. Clearly, government contactors should strive to increase their 7-Factor scores since the modest investment can produce large payoffs in new business revenue.

We also found that on average companies in the government market had 17% higher 7-Factor scores and 28% higher win rates than companies in the commercial space.

Perhaps government-market win rates track more closely to the quality of capture and proposal work, whereas commercial proposals are more broadly influenced by brand marketing.

Predicting your return on investment

As a general rule, your win rate percentage will increase point for point with the increase in your 7-Factor score. This rule applies to companies that develop enough proposals each year that they have a good proposal team,

Best Informed Wins
Collected Articles of Bob Lohfeld from
Washington Technology (2010 – 2012)

some established processes, and are doing reasonably well winning their share of bids.

Your company needs to have enough proposal volume to produce an economic payoff for making the investments. Your company also needs to have a reasonable win rate established as a starting point.

If you have a very low win rate, there may be other serious problems that need to be fixed before you fine-tune your business-acquisition efforts.

Here's what a typical company might expect. (Stick with me because there is some math here, but I promise nothing more complicated than multiplication and division.)

A typical government contractor graduating from the small business program might have $40 million a year in revenue, a 30% win rate, and a 16 for its 7-Factor score.

Let's assume the company must generate $20 million in replacement revenue just to stay even and wants to grow revenue by 20% ($8 million) next year. To do this, the company must have $28 million in new revenue next year.

If awarded contracts have a nominal 5-year period of performance, then the company has to win $140 million in new business. If its win rate is 30%, and the win rate doesn't drop after graduation, then the company has to bid $466 million to produce $28 million in new revenue next year.

Now assume that the company selects investments that will raise its 7-Factor score by 20% with the expectation that this will result in a 20% increase in its win rate. Increasing the win rate by 20% means the win rate will go from 30% to 36%. This will produce additional revenue equal to 6% of all bids the company makes.

In this example, 6% of $466 million is an additional $30 million in revenue. If the marginal profit rate is 5%, the investments would drop $1.5 million to the company's bottom line.

From a shareholder perspective, the additional $30 million in new business spread across a 5-year period of performance would bump up revenue by $6 million next year and could increase shareholder value by the same amount, assuming shares are valued at 1 times revenue.

Now compute the ROI. Assuming our example company needs to make $200 thousand in investments to raise the 7-Factor score by 20%, and the revenue increase produced an additional $1.5 million to the bottom line, then the ROI ratio would be 7.5 to 1. I believe this is called a *no brainer*.

Make the investments and move on to enjoy your newfound prosperity.

WashingtonTechnology.com, January 5, 2012

Best Informed Wins
Collected Articles of Bob Lohfeld from
Washington Technology **(2010 – 2012)**

3 tips to maximize past performance

Take advantage of this predictor of how well you'll perform

Almost every proposal you write has a requirement for information on past performance. The government uses this information to evaluate how well your company has performed on similar programs and expects your past performance to be a predictor of how well you will perform on the program you're currently bidding.

Because past performance can be an important discriminator in the evaluation and selection process, there are some things you should know about how to write your past performance response.

Past performance versus past experience

Past performance comprises a set of specific contracts that you select to demonstrate how well your company, or your team, has performed on contracts that are similar in size, scope, and complexity to your current bid.

Past experience, which is sometimes confused with past performance, is about the broader issue of what experience and expertise the bidding organization has gained from all of its contract work and the work of its teammates.

Select contracts to demonstrate past performance

Past performance is all about relevancy and how well you performed the work you're referencing. The government will consider these two factors together when developing your past-performance score—and both are important. However, performance is more important than relevancy. It is better to showcase your best-performing contracts and argue that they are relevant than to select contracts that are highly relevant and had poor performance.

Best Informed Wins
Collected Articles of Bob Lohfeld from *Washington Technology* (2010 – 2012)

Expect the government evaluator to ask your customers how well you did performing each contract. Typically, this happens via a formal past-performance questionnaire submission process and/or direct communication from the government evaluators to your customers. The government keeps two databases—the Contractor Performance Assessment Reporting System (CPARS) and Past Performance Information Retrieval System (PPIRS)—to determine how well your company performs its contracts.

Government access is restricted to those individuals who are working on source selections, to include contractor responsibility determinations.

With the CPARS, companies can regularly review their own ratings for each evaluated contract, but cannot check ratings for other companies. In order to access PPIRS information, a contractor must be registered in the Central Contractor Registration (CCR) system and must have created a Marketing Partner Identification Number (MPIN) in the CCR profile. Because past-performance ratings are such an important factor in proposal evaluations, every company should regularly review its CPARS ratings and challenge any evaluations they consider unfair.

Write your past performance summary

Each RFP will be very prescriptive about the information you need to provide when you describe each past-performance contract. While it may seem obvious, you really do need to provide all the requested information in order to submit a *compliant* proposal (see my article, *6 reasons your proposals fail*).

You'll be asked to provide information to show contract relevance, so keep this in mind when you write your response. Measures of relevance include contract size, scope and complexity, as well as the technical scope of work performed.

The description of the work is where you can stand out. Write your response to not only show that you performed relevant work—which every bidder does—but that you also had specific accomplishments that were meaningful to the government. Don't just parrot back the statement of work from the contract you are citing. Focus on accomplishments because it's these achievements that can make your contract past performance stand out from the crowd.

Most importantly, make sure you have outstanding past performance on the contracts you present. Confirm this information with your customers and with your teammates' customers before you submit your proposal.

The government will read what you write, and they will validate the content. A good writer can present your past performance in a credible, compelling way, but if the underlying performance is less than desirable, it's hard to overcome the truth.

WashingtonTechnology.com, February 10, 2012

Best Informed Wins
Collected Articles of Bob Lohfeld from
Washington Technology (2010 – 2012)

How to avoid a contract protest

Are protests destined to become just one more milestone in the federal procurement process?

Are protests destined to become just one more milestone in the federal procurement process? Recent evidence might suggest so. Notably, the protested award to Lockheed Martin for the U.S. Antarctic Research program in the South Pole and the Hawker Beechcraft protest of the award of the new light attack aircraft trainer are recent examples.

In addition, market experts predict that as defense budgets decline, companies fighting over fewer dollars will launch more protests when losing procurements that can lock them out of programs or agencies for a decade.

Best Informed Wins
Collected Articles of Bob Lohfeld from *Washington Technology* (2010 – 2012)

If protests are to become the norm for competing in major programs, then it's to everyone's advantage to find ways to reduce the number of protests and awards that are overturned. When companies file protests, everyone loses. The procuring agency loses because procurement time lines get stretched out. Bidders lose because the cost of participating in federal procurements goes up. Even the apparent winner incurs additional costs to defend the award, and the losing bidders incur additional costs to file the protest.

Capture and proposal managers can take some precautions that may help minimize the likelihood that their procurement will be protested or award overturned. To learn first-hand what you can do, I reached out to three attorneys with practices in federal procurement protests to see what they suggest. Here's what I learned.

According to Dave Nadler, a partner at Dickstein Shapiro LLP in Washington, DC, protests can begin when the government releases a defective request for proposals. "Review the RFP with an eye to unclear, ambiguous, unduly restrictive text, especially text specifying a brand name or written around someone else's product. It is better to seek clarification and use the Q&A process to make sure the solicitation is clear and that your interpretation is reasonable than to file a protest," he said.

If you are unclear about the interpretation of proposal instructions (typically section L) or the evaluation criteria (typically section M), then the evaluation team will probably be confused too. If the RFP is deficient, and you choose to protest the RFP, then you must file your protest before your proposal is submitted, otherwise the Government Accountability Office will rule that your protest is untimely and will summarily dismiss it, Nadler said.

As a proposal writer, there is nothing more frustrating than working with a poorly written RFP. If you have one of these, let me know and I'll present your argument to the agency pro bono for the good of our industry. We will all benefit from well-written RFPs.

As you write your proposal, there are other pitfalls to avoid. Shlomo Katz, counsel at Brown Rudnick LLP, reinforces that you must follow the requirement of the RFP precisely. "If the RFP requires certain documentation (e.g., resumes) or certain credentials (e.g., a Ph.D.), and you don't provide what was required, and the agency selects you anyway, that may be grounds for a successful protest. Similarly, if you make technical claims back them up with data, especially if you are claiming your widget is twice as good, twice as fast, twice as durable, etc. Ditto if you claim you can deliver in half the time of your competitors. Explain your technical approach in sufficient detail to justify that you are the best (if that's what the evaluation criteria call for)," said Katz.

You can also have protests related to your proposed costs. According to Katz, "If your cost/price is significantly higher than your competition, make sure you explain the value proposition, and if your cost/price is significantly lower than your competition, make sure you explain why it is realistic. I had a protest where the agency selected the offeror whose cost was way below the government estimate, and GAO threw out the award because the proposal did not prove its own cost realism."

There are also some legal gotchas, according to Carol L. O'Riordan, partner in the O'Riordan Bethel Law Firm, LLP. "Ensure that everyone on the team has current and required licensing, credentials, and past performance in place because it is more than embarrassing if a subcontractor's employee is put forth as key personnel, but his required license is outdated or lapsed," O'Riordan said. "If the procurement uses GSA schedule vehicles, make sure the team's vehicles include the required services. Watch out for organizational conflicts of interest. Starting with all known information regarding the procurement and evaluation, make sure you understand to what extent everyone on the proposed team checked and confirmed that each has no affiliation or involvement with those identified on the other side or other procurements where conflicts may exist."

As a final thought, some protests can be brought to the procuring agency for review, rather than going directly to GAO. This may be more advantageous, but be mindful that there are certainly timeliness rules that apply to whichever protest venue you choose.

WashingtonTechnology.com, March 22, 2012

Best Informed Wins
Collected Articles of Bob Lohfeld from
Washington Technology **(2010 – 2012)**

6 quick fixes that will improve your company's win rate

We're frequently asked how to improve a company's overall win rate, and I outlined these in the article I wrote in my January 2012 column, *How to raise your win rate by 20 percent*, using our seven-factor model. Since then, we've been surveying companies to see how well they perform in these seven factors and to identify areas where companies can make immediate improvements.

In this article, I'll share some of the survey results and show you immediate actions you can take to help raise your company's overall win rate.

In February and March 2012, we conducted two surveys—one with the Association of Proposal Management Professionals (APMP) and the other with the Deltek GovCon team. The surveys asked proposal managers, capture managers, and business development professionals to rate how well their companies performed in each of the seven factors. We used 28 questions in the survey to measure performance and to pinpoint areas where companies could make improvements to raise their win rates. Based on the survey, here are six quick fixes that most companies can make to improve their win rates.

1. Capture and proposal training

Only 52% of the companies surveyed provide career development and professional training for their business development, capture management, and proposal development staffs.

Every company should have career development plans for its employees and offer professional development training for its management, key employees, and especially for those people involved in business development, capture management, and proposal development. They should also provide training in proposal writing for technical and managerial professionals to help them write more compelling proposals.

Companies can develop these training programs internally or contract the training to companies that provide such specialized training. However you do it, some training is better than no training. By offering this kind of training, you can immediately leapfrog half the companies in your market.

2. Business acquisition process

Of the companies surveyed, 54% have not documented their business acquisition processes.

It is an indisputable principle that having a well-structured business acquisition process increases business acquisition effectiveness and reduces cost, yet half the companies surveyed compete using undocumented processes. Documenting these processes is the first step in raising the maturity of the business acquisition process. All companies of any reasonable size should have defined, repeatable businesses acquisition processes covering the business development, capture, pre-proposal preparation, proposal development, and post-proposal submission phases of the business acquisition life cycle. These processes should be fully supported by management and used for all new business acquisition.

3. Capture management

Only 33% of companies review their capture progress and use these reviews to make management decisions about pursuing or continuing to pursue new business opportunities.

Companies should evaluate every new business pursuit monthly and make an affirmative decision to continue, delay, or suspend the pursuit. If no reviews are conducted, then every new business opportunity remains in play, even when it is clear that the company can't win. Proper capture management reduces the effort spent on opportunities that are likely to be *losers* and focuses effort on opportunities with a better chance of winning. Measuring capture progress and making associated management decisions also are essential parts of the business acquisition process and necessary for increasing your win rate.

4. Management decisions

Only 45% of companies surveyed use gate reviews as part of their business acquisition process.

Best Informed Wins
Collected Articles of Bob Lohfeld from *Washington Technology* (2010 – 2012)

The purpose of gate reviews is to ensure that management makes timely decisions about continuing to invest in a new business opportunity and to provide an opportunity for executive management to coach the capture team on how to raise its win probability. These gate reviews are fundamental to effective and efficient acquisition of new business.

5. Annotated outlines

Seventy percent of proposal writers begin writing their assigned sections before management has approved what they are going to write.

Annotated outlines or storyboards probably are not used. If they are used, they are not reviewed and approved by management. No wonder there is so much rewriting involved in completing typical proposals.

6. Proposal quality

Thirty seven percent of companies surveyed said their proposals suffer from errors that could cause them to lose bids.

Professionally developed proposals do not have these problems. They are always compliant, compelling, and responsive. Major improvements in proposal quality are still needed by many companies.

Compete survey results are available on our website.

WashingtonTechnology.com, April 23, 2012

Best Informed Wins
Collected Articles of Bob Lohfeld from *Washington Technology* (2010 – 2012)

Can you keep your bid out of the reject box?

I was asked to review one of the proposals submitted for the first stage of the Army's multi-billion dollar *Army Eagle* logistics procurement and to advise an unsuccessful bidder why the company had failed to make the cut. My answer was straightforward—the bidder failed to write a proposal for the evaluators to evaluate. Here's how the proposal went wrong.

Army Eagle is a multiple award procurement for large and small businesses that is being competed in stages. The first-stage submission, which I reviewed, was an advisory stage that required bidders to submit a short proposal describing their understanding of the Army's logistics program and how their team's capabilities and resources could help fulfill that mission. Based on this response, the Army advised bidders whether their team might be successful should they decide to proceed to stage 2 of the competition, the submission of a full proposal. Stage 1 was an advisory stage and does not preclude a bidder from proceeding to stage 2 even if the Army advises that the bidder is unlikely to win.

How evaluators evaluate

To write a great, short proposal, it's helpful to imagine how your proposal is likely to be evaluated. In this case, you might visualize evaluators sitting at a large table. At one end of the table are stacks of proposals, and at the other end are two boxes—one for proposals that are likely to be successful and the other for proposals that are likely to be unsuccessful.

You might further imagine that the evaluators have agreed upon a standard for reviewing and scoring these proposals. In this case, the standard would certainly include how well the bidders explained their understanding of the Army's logistics strategy and how well their team's experience and resources stacked up against that mission. You should expect that a scoring template would be used to evaluate each proposal and serve as a basis for sorting the proposals into the appropriate box.

Quick look assessment

As a proposal professional, you know that when evaluators have multiple proposals to review, they will read and evaluate them in three passes. The first pass is a quick look to make sure that your Eagle proposal followed the RFP instructions. They want to see that you titled sections as expected and structured your proposal so that content appears where it is expected to be. Every proposal should pass this quick-look compliance test and, assuming your proposal does, the evaluator will perform the second evaluation pass.

Proposal content skimming

The second pass comprises proposal content skimming. Here you would expect the evaluator to flip through the pages more slowly, looking at the figures and tables and reading the action captions that go with data presented graphically in each proposal section. This pass is like reading a graphic novel with the reader looking at the pictures and expecting the story to be told without having to read the text.

To score well, your Eagle proposal's first section should have an insightful graphic depicting the bidder's understanding of the

Army's logistics mission. The next sections, on experience and resources, should have well-crafted data tables proving relevant team experience and resources with action captions explaining how this data relates to fulfilling the Army's mission. If crafted correctly, the content-skimming pass should establish a solid first impression that your proposal is a winner and should be sufficient for the evaluator to develop an initial score for your proposal. After content skimming, the evaluator should have a pretty good idea which of the two boxes your proposal is destined for.

Detailed proposal reading

The third pass is the detailed reading of the proposal text. With the evaluator having developed an expectation from the figures and tables about what the text will convey, the evaluator is now ready to delve deeper into the proposal and understand the full story conveyed by the text. The text should reinforce the story that was told through the graphical presentation and point out any subtleties the evaluator may have missed while skimming figures and tables. The text ties it all together and completes the story.

Best Informed Wins
Collected Articles of Bob Lohfeld from *Washington Technology* (2010 – 2012)

In reviewing the unsuccessful bidder's proposal, I found no content to evaluate in the content-skimming second pass. The proposal had no figures and only one data table that was poorly constructed. Content skimming put this proposal solidly in the loser category, and the text did not redeem the offeror.

Upon reflection, I think the bidder had a good team and could have been successful in the stage 1 competition, but the proposal document lost the game.

WashingtonTechnology.com, May 16, 2012

Will low-price contracting make us all losers?

We are seeing a procurement strategy shift for technical and professional services bids brought about by procurement officials using lowest price, technically acceptable (LPTA) evaluation criteria rather than the more traditional best-value tradeoff criteria.

While there is certainly a place for the low-price strategy in federal procurements, it is definitely not suitable for procurements with complex services or uncertain performance risk. When the government applies the strategy to unsuitable procurements, both the government and the bidders lose. Here's what happens and what you can do about it.

Best Informed Wins
Collected Articles of Bob Lohfeld from
Washington Technology (2010 – 2012)

When to use LPTA evaluation criteria

LPTA is actually a form of best value. In traditional best value procurements, the government allows tradeoffs among non-cost factors such as technical approach, management plan, past performance, etc. and cost when determining best value to the government. These tradeoffs give the government the latitude to award a contract to other than the lowest priced offeror when the tradeoffs show there is additional value to the government in these factors. When selecting the LPTA criteria for procurements, the government determines before the release of the request for proposals (RFP) that there is no additional value in trading off the non-cost factors versus cost.

In fact, LPTA evaluations specifically prohibit evaluators from making these tradeoffs and restrict evaluators to only scoring proposal factors and subfactors as either acceptable or unacceptable. The result is there is no value in the bidder exceeding any requirement in the RFP.

DOD's Source Selection Procedure is prescriptive about when it is appropriate to use LPTA. "The LPTA process is appropriate when best value is expected to result from selection of a technically acceptable proposal with the lowest evaluated price. LPTA may be used in situations where the government would not realize any value from a proposal exceeding the government's minimum technical or performance requirements, often for acquisitions of commercial or non-complex services or supplies which are clearly defined and expected to be low risk."

Procurements can use a hybrid of the tradeoff and LPTA approaches. For example, an RFP might state that the offeror's small and small disadvantaged business subcontracting plan is evaluated as acceptable or unacceptable, while the technical approach is evaluated as being a best-value tradeoff based on the technical evaluation factor and subfactors. This can be a good compromise for some procurements since the hybrid approach lets evaluators trade off important proposal considerations against cost while using a pass/fail criteria for less important considerations.

Setting minimum technical and performance requirements

Procurements get into trouble when the LPTA criteria is applied to technical and professional services bids because the work is complex, minimum acceptable technical and performance requirements are difficult to describe, and the consequences from failure can be considerable.

In LPTA procurements, setting higher standards for acceptability becomes important because each bidder who meets the minimum acceptable standards has an equal opportunity to be selected for contract award. Setting the standards too low will let marginally acceptable bidders become candidates for contract award. These are the same bidders who would normally have been weeded out in best-value tradeoff procurements.

If standards are too low, every bidder will get through the acceptable hurdle, leaving only cost as the evaluation factor. Low standards effectively transform an LPTA procurement into an invitation for bid where award is made solely on the basis of price. These are inappropriate for professional and technical services bids.

Ideally, an RFP will define acceptability standards high enough to prevent marginal bidders from becoming candidates for award. To do this, an RFP must describe all requirements in a way that an evaluator can clearly determine what constitutes the higher level of acceptability and then differentiate between acceptable and unacceptable proposals. In services bids, it is often difficult enough to define the requirements, let alone define what constitutes an appropriately high level of acceptability for each factor or subfactor.

Raising standards of acceptability

To raise the standards of acceptability, an RFP might prescribe that the bidder have CMMI or ISO certifications or require proposed key or technical staff to have specific undergraduate degrees, advanced degrees, and/or professional certifications.

I've seen LPTA procurements where the incumbent's program manager failed to meet the minimum educational requirements, and the company bid the program manager anyway because he was well liked—only to discover later that their bid was determined to be unacceptable and they lost the competition because they did not meet this almost arbitrary personnel requirement.

Best Informed Wins
Collected Articles of Bob Lohfeld from
Washington Technology **(2010 – 2012)**

Past performance might require evidence of several completed contracts of a minimum size or completed within the past 12 months. If the bidder doesn't meet these requirements, they must be evaluated as unacceptable.

Interestingly, DOD again prescribes, "when applying LPTA criteria to past performance evaluations, an offeror without a record of relevant past performance or for whom information on past performance is not available or is so sparse that no meaningful past performance rating can be reasonably assigned, the offeror may not be evaluated favorably or unfavorably on past performance (see FAR 15.305 (a)(2)(iv)). Therefore, the offeror shall be determined to have unknown past performance. In the context of acceptability/unacceptability, unknown shall be considered acceptable."

Each higher requirement raises the bar of acceptability, but because the evaluation is LPTA, the government cannot give additional consideration to companies exceeding a requirement by considerable margin over those who squeak by, barely meeting the requirement.

If it's not easy to clearly define higher criteria for acceptability, then it's best to avoid LPTA and use traditional best-value tradeoffs.

Lowest price wins

When an offeror's proposal has been found acceptable, all that stands between the offeror and victory is having the lowest evaluated price. Bidders use many tactics to lower their evaluated price. With the application of these tactics, each bidder takes on more risk in contract performance. Generally, as price is pushed downward, performance risk goes up.

The satisfaction of having awarded to the lowest price offeror can soon be overshadowed by the burden of poor contractor performance. Slow contract staffing is an early indicator of contractor performance problems, followed by marginal technical accomplishment, late deliveries, and ultimately cost overruns. In the long run, the lowest bidder's performance reputation suffers, and the government is criticized for cost and schedule overruns and for failing to manage their program correctly. In the end, everyone loses.

We can all avoid this plight if we all help educate program and procurement officials about pitfalls of using LPTA as a procurement strategy for technical and professional services bids.

WashingtonTechnology.com, June 4, 2012

Best Informed Wins
Collected Articles of Bob Lohfeld from
Washington Technology (2010 – 2012)

100 words that kill your proposals

Inexperienced proposal writers seem to use words that should be avoided when writing proposals. These inappropriate words and phrases can weaken a proposal, annoy evaluators, and even undermine the bidder's credibility.

To help you write better proposals, we have compiled a list of the most frequently used words that should be avoided when writing proposals. Some of these came from Carl Dickson at CapturePlanning.com, while others came from lists that have circulated around the proposal industry for so long that the identity of the original authors has been lost.

Our list doesn't cover every word that should be avoided, and there are certainly exceptions to the usage rules, but our list does provide guidance and suggests alternative words that will strengthen your proposal. (The full list is actually about 200 words.)

Here's a brief discussion of the kinds of words you should avoid.

Crutch words

When writers don't know what to say, they often use crutch words to make the reader think they know what they are writing about. For example, when a proposal writer says, "We understand your requirements," then fails to demonstrate any understanding, the writer is using the word *understand* as a crutch.

The proposal would be much stronger if the writer demonstrated an understanding of the requirements by discussing how features of their proposal fulfill customer requirements. Avoid using the word *understand* in your proposal. It will most certainly be a crutch that replaces what should be a discussion of your understanding.

Boasting words

Boasting words cause a proposal to lose credibility and undermine the integrity of the bidder. I know every 10-person company feels compelled to say they are *world class, uniquely*

Best Informed Wins
Collected Articles of Bob Lohfeld from
Washington Technology (2010 – 2012)

qualified, use best-of-breed tools, have industry-standard processes, have state-of-the-art technology, and are *thought leaders in their market.*

I can assure you no proposal evaluator has ever based an award decision on this kind of puffery. Remove boasting words from your proposal, and focus your proposal on what you are going to do for the customer, instead of trying to make your firm sound so important. Interestingly, the bigger and more successful companies are, the more humble they seem to be about their credentials.

Vague, useless words

No proposal evaluator has ever been moved by a proposal that said we are pleased to submit this proposal, enthusiastic about performing this work, committed to top quality, or we place our customers first. These are just useless words in a proposal. You will do better if you strip these from your proposal, and write about what matters—which is how you are going to do the work.

Weak, timid words

We believe, think, feel, strive, attempt, intend, etc. are all words that contemplate failure to perform as an acceptable outcome. Say what you intend to do, and don't couch it in timid terms.

Redundant words

In page-limited proposals, concise writing is mandatory. Let's make it a practice to replace redundant words with precise words. For example, replace *actual experience* with *experience*, *advanced planning* with *planning*, *close proximity* with *proximity*, *consensus of opinion* with *consensus*, and so on.

Unnecessary qualifiers

We are absolutely certain, it goes without saying, now and again, comparatively, thoroughly, needless to say, etc. are unnecessary qualifiers. While these words and many similar words may have a place in proposals, most writers use them as unnecessary qualifiers. Remove them to make your writing more concise.

Needlessly long words

Normally, you wouldn't use unnecessarily long words in conversation, so there's no need to use them in a proposal. Replace *ascertain* with *learn*, *encompass* with *include*, *enumerate* with *list*, *illustrate* with *show*, *initiate* with *start*, and so on.

Slang

We are hitting the ground running and rolling out the red carpet with seasoned managers... You might say this in conversation and it would be fine, but in a proposal, it just sounds odd. Proposals are more formal and may even end up being part of the contract, so write without using slang.

If I've missed some of your favorite words to avoid, let me know and I'll add them to the long list on our website.

WashingtonTechnology.com, July 20, 2012

4 Keys to better capture analytics

And 7 ways to measure the quality of your pursuit decisions...

Capture analytics is the science of measuring how well you have performed each of the activities in your capture management process and then correlating these measurements with the outcomes of your bids.

Understanding this correlation can help you make better decisions about what deals to pursue and how likely you are to win, and they can improve the accuracy of your revenue predictions.

The foundation for capture analytics is econometrics, which uses statistical techniques to isolate the degree to which each activity in the capture process contributes to the win. It takes a lot of historical data to do this correlation well, but when done correctly, it can become a powerful predictor of win rates and new business revenue.

So how does it work and how can you use capture analytics to your advantage?

Measuring capture performance

Capture management is a process that has a defined set of activities to be performed for every capture you do. Your capture team should follow a documented, repeatable process on every capture and make fundamental measurements of how well they are performing each activity in the capture process.

Making measurements provides a quantitative basis for assessing and optimizing your capture process. With measurement, you have a basis to improve your process; without it, you are just guessing.

You already use measurements in the proposal development process. When you do color reviews, everyone understands what you mean when you say the draft management section of a proposal gets a red score. These color scores are measures of the quality of your proposal.

Best Informed Wins
Collected Articles of Bob Lohfeld from *Washington Technology* (2010 – 2012)

These same color measures can be used to measure quality in the capture phase and give you a consistent framework for measuring performance across your full business acquisition life cycle.

Measuring the quality of your pursuit decisions

The pursuit decision is the first decision in the capture management process. It is the decision that is made to establish a capture team and fund the capture effort. I like to use seven factors to evaluate how well this decision is made. If a good decision is made, you'll probably win, and if it was not so good, you'll probably lose.

Here are the seven factors I use to assess the quality of the pursuit decision. You can modify these factors or use your own. What is important is that you establish evaluation factors and measure how well the deal lines up against them.

1. **Customer knowledge.** Do we know the customer, their mission, issues, concerns, preferences, requirements, goals, etc. and if we don't, is there a

good chance we can discover these during the capture process?

2. **Right solution.** Do we have the solution the customer wants to buy, or can we create that solution during the capture process?

3. **Customer advocacy.** Does the customer know us, our management team, our past performance, our reputation for doing outstanding work, etc., and is there a sense that the customer is favorable to our performing the work?

4. **Competition.** How much competition will we face, and do we believe we can overcome these competitors?

5. **Win strategy.** Do we have (or can we create) an acceptable win strategy?

6. **Financials.** What is it going to cost to take on this pursuit and proposal effort and to start up the contract? What is the expected profit if we perform the contract well? Is this a good financial decision?

7. **Capture/proposal resources.** Do we have (or can we get) the resources to conduct an effective capture campaign and write a winning proposal?

I rate each of these evaluation factors using the same blue, green, yellow, and red color scores that we use to evaluate proposal quality.

Hopefully, you have been documenting color scores for all your pursuit decisions made during the year and now have collected enough data in your capture analytics effort to begin looking at results.

Pursuit decision factor evaluations typically start out being fairly subjective, but over time, you can define what constitutes each color rating, and the ratings will become more objective and consistent. For example, *customer knowledge from face-to-face meetings* generally gets a higher rating than *customer knowledge gained from reading websites*. If you document the basis for each assessment, you will become objective and consistent in your measurements.

Predicting wins and losses

You will find there is an amazing correlation between the color scores in your pursuit decision, capture progress, and your win/loss outcome. When your pursuit factors are scored and you have more greens and blues in these scores, the data will show that you are more likely to win. The more reds and yellows, the more likely you are to lose. And the more data you have, the more confidence you'll have in your predictions.

The mathematics behind this is called multivariate regression analysis. If you want to do these calculations, get someone with a good statistical background to set up the equations. It is not that hard to do, and you can set it up in Excel, but the tasking is intimidating to the novice.

Making effective management decisions

With data, management can make better decisions about pursuits and can do a better job picking winners out of all those deals your business development team wants to pursue.

Capture analytics is a tool to help management make better, more consistent decisions. It is an advisory tool and does not replace management judgment. Correlation is a statistical prediction process based on historical data, and individual pursuits might not fit the historical data used to make the correlation. For example, making a decision to pursue a program with red and yellow pursuit factor scores can be a good management decision provided there is a very high payoff and low investment; however, I would caution that you don't want this to become the norm for your company. Another example is when you have red and yellow pursuit factor scores and still pursue a deal because you expect the government use lowest price, technically acceptable (LPTA) evaluation criteria. It makes sense to use a different set of pursuit factors for LPTA procurements since the standard for technical acceptability is low.

Using capture analytics will make you a better manager and a better decision-maker and help you deliver on the revenue promises you make each year to your shareholders.

Making the pursuit decision is one of the most important capture decisions an executive can make. If you have made these decisions well over the past year, you should be enjoying a winning season and be on target to deliver the revenue your shareholders are expecting. If you made these decisions poorly, you will

Best Informed Wins
Collected Articles of Bob Lohfeld from
Washington Technology **(2010 – 2012)**

probably be looking for a new job as you read this article.

WashingtonTechnology.com, August 29, 2012

Do's and don'ts of lowering your proposal costs

I used to think that no one would have the audacity to say you're spending too much on proposals as long as you were winning.

With companies falling short of revenue goals, however, most certainly there will be downward pressure on all operating costs, including proposals costs. There are easily 50 ways to reduce proposal costs, but regrettably, 45 of these will also lower your win rate.

The challenge is to reduce proposal costs without reducing your win rate.

We have done a lot of work on win rates and ways to reduce proposal costs. Here are some ideas that work and some that don't.

Compensation levels for proposal professionals

With few exceptions, reducing proposal costs is all about reducing the total amount of labor needed to create a winning proposal, not reducing the hourly rate paid to the workforce. In the proposal field, you pretty much get what you pay for, so hiring low-priced labor tends to create a workforce that works slowly and suffers from proposal quality issues.

Generally, you can overcome these quality issues by applying additional hours for proposal rework, but this runs up the total cost. In the end, setting hiring salaries below market norms will likely increase the total cost of proposals. Even worse, outsourcing proposals to low-cost offshore providers has just not worked in the Federal Government arena.

Let's resolve that the first step in reducing proposal costs is to hire good proposal professionals who are highly productive at their profession and pay a fair wage for these professionals. The Association of Proposal Management Professionals (APMP) conducts a study on salaries of proposal professionals worldwide, and the newly released 2012 study can be a good starting point to help you assess your salaries' competitiveness.

70/30 proposal staffing rule

Managing your proposal staff's downtime is another area to examine when reducing proposal costs. When there is a lull in the workload, the company is still paying salaries, benefits, and other costs for proposal employees with little derived benefit. Because government solicitations arrive when the government wants to release them and not when we are ready to write them, there will always be peaks and valleys in proposal workloads, and this creates times when the in-house proposal team is paid to sit on the bench.

You can reduce this bench cost by staffing your internal proposal team to handle about 70% of the expected annual proposal workload and then contracting out the remaining 30% as peaks occur. Using this just-in-time, 70/30 proposal staffing strategy will save money in the long-run even considering that you probably pay more per hour for external resources. If you have any doubt about this, look at what it costs to staff up with your in-house team for an imminent RFP and then to keep that army of resources in place while the RFP slips month after month. It will make you a believer in the 70/30 rule.

Processes, tools, and training

It should come as no surprise that you can make capital investments that will increase your proposal workforce's productivity. Higher productivity equates to fewer hours required to produce proposals. Trading capital investment for labor is well understood and one of the best ways to reduce overall labor costs.

In the proposal area, these kinds of investments generally pay for themselves within 12 months. Some of our favorite investments include processes, tools, and professional training. If you haven't already done so, consider standardizing and documenting your proposal processes for task orders and larger proposals based on industry best practice models. Establish a collaborative enterprise repository for use in managing all your proposal development activities. Use collaborative tools such as GoToMeeting or WebEx as part of your proposal tool suite. Keep computer and office software up to date (SharePoint 2010, Office 2010, Adobe CS6,

SnagIt 11, Mindjet MindManager 2012, WinZip 16.5, etc.), and make sure you use the many low-cost and free software tools that improve personal proposal productivity. We evaluate these tools and publish a list of over 100 of our favorites on our Lohfeld Consulting Group website.

You should invest in other productivity tools as well, including:

- An online proposal library of your past proposals and RFPs.

- A resume database of all resumes you've used in proposals and resumes of all your professional employees.

- A project past performance database of all the contracts that you are likely to cite in your proposals, including write-ups about what you actually accomplished when performing these contracts.

- An online graphics library of reusable proposal graphics.

- A library of pre-written proposal content covering such topics as your project management plan, recruiting process, accounting processes, etc. so you can use these in proposals.

Proposal travel costs

Travel costs also figure into the overall costs of doing proposals. You can reduce these costs by teleworking and by running proposals in a virtual development environment. The Washington, DC beltway is jammed with people commuting to and from work each day. If you allow telework on proposals, you can convert commute time into productive proposal time.

Companies frequently use out-of-town travel to bring large teams together to work on proposals. Putting them up in hotels and paying travel and meal expenses can add up. Some companies insist this is necessary to do their proposals, while others with dispersed workforces regularly develop proposals virtually.

Virtual proposal development using the right tools is highly effective and cost efficient. In our case, we manage virtual proposal development for some companies where we have never met anyone face-to-face. We manage the entire process using proposal

Best Informed Wins
Collected Articles of Bob Lohfeld from *Washington Technology* **(2010 – 2012)**

collaboration tools, and the proposals are just as good as if everyone had traveled to a central location to work the proposal.

There are many other cost-saving tips that we did not discuss. I'm sure you also have your favorite cost-saving tips. If you would like to share them so others can learn from your experiences, email them to me at *RLohfeld@LohfeldConsulting.com.*

WashingtonTechnology.com, September 27, 2012

Best Informed Wins
Collected Articles of Bob Lohfeld from
Washington Technology (2010 – 2012)

7 steps from good to great proposals

A win doesn't always mean what you submitted was the best it could be

We all strive to write great proposals and often pat ourselves on the back when our proposals win. Each victory fills us with pride and reassures us that we're writing great proposals, but that's not always the case.

Great proposals frequently lose on price, and poorly written proposals win when competition is limited or the bid price is low. Because of this, victory is not always a good indicator of proposal quality.

All great proposals have seven essential attributes, and you can use these attributes to measure the quality of your proposal. Once you make it a practice to measure these attributes, you'll be surprised at how quickly all of your proposals improve.

To be a great proposal, a proposal must embody the following.

1. Compliant structure

First and foremost, the proposal must be structured to comply exactly with the request for proposals (RFP) instructions and attachments, thereby making it easy for an evaluator to identify which sections of the proposal correspond to each RFP instruction. All requested topics should be easily found in the proposal outline. Additionally, the proposal outline must provide a place for all information needed to evaluate the proposal. When this information is not requested in the instructions, provide additional sections in the proposal outline so these sections can be mapped easily to the proposal evaluation criteria.

2. Responsive content

Each section of the proposal must fully address what is asked for in the RFP instructions and evaluation criteria. Responsive content must focus on how your company will do the work, not just delineate the work to be done. Sections must address the required topics and not introduce other topics that are not relevant to the subject.

3. Customer focused

The proposal must present your vision of what you are going to do for the customer in a way that makes the customer feel they will be better off with you as their contractor. Place your emphasis on the customer, not you the bidder. Customers always want to read about how the bidder is going to apply its expertise to improve the work and results by providing faster, better, cheaper approaches. They don't want to read bragging statements about how great the bidder is.

4. Compelling and feature rich

Your solution must be presented in such a way that it has many features that will be evaluated as *proposal strengths*. Features, and their associated benefits, will be scored as strengths because they increase the likelihood of successful mission accomplishment or exceed a contract requirement. Without these features and benefits, a proposal can never be compelling. Be careful to substantiate each feature and its associated benefit with evidence or proof such as providing metrics, quantitative data, etc., otherwise these may be viewed as just fabricated features without any real expected benefit. The proposal must provide a sufficient number of strengths to compel the customer to make the award to your firm.

5. Easy to evaluate

Features of your proposal that you want scored as proposal strengths should be easy to discover by a sleepy evaluator. Showcase these features, tables, and graphics, or use icons so these features stand out from the rest of your proposal. Make it virtually impossible for an evaluator to miss your proposal strengths.

6. Visual communications

The proposal must be attractive, but more importantly, must use visual communications (graphics, tables, icons) to tell your story and present your features that will be scored as strengths. Some evaluators will skim your proposal looking at paragraph headers, tables, and graphics, and they will score your proposal initially on what they see through visual communications. Other evaluators will read text and ignore graphics. A great proposal can be scored by proposal skimmers as well as proposal readers. Use visual communications to bring out the features that will give you a good evaluation score.

7. Well written

The proposal must avoid empty words, be written concisely, convey just what you want the reader to understand, and avoid using the 100+ words that can kill your proposal. (See my article *100 words that kill your proposals*.)

For each proposal, I like to evaluate all seven attributes using a red, yellow, green, and blue color score. You can build a simple matrix listing the seven attributes down the left side of the matrix and across the top of the matrix list your normal color reviews (pink team, red team, gold team, etc.). Ask your proposal review team to color score each of the seven attributes when they do their normal color reviews.

When you do this, two things will happen. First, the writers and reviewers will focus on moving proposal quality higher since everyone wants to receive a blue score for each of the seven attributes. You should see a strong trend showing proposal quality improvement as you go through your normal review cycles. Second, you will have a good quantitative measure of the quality of your proposals, and you can correlate proposal quality with your wins to prove that high-quality proposals have a higher win rate.

Everyone knows that you can't manage what you can't measure. With a good set of proposal quality measures, you can manage proposal quality, and with good proposal quality management, you will see all your proposals and your win rates improve.

WashingtonTechnology.com, October 24, 2012

Today's market demands benchmarking proposals—here's how

Advice on how to benchmark your proposals and increase your win-rates

I attended a session on proposal benchmarking at the Association of Proposal Management Professionals, National Capital Area Chapter's (APMP-NCA), Mid Atlantic Proposal Conference & Exhibition a few months ago and was surprised to learn how few companies actually benchmark the quality of their proposals or the capabilities of their proposal departments.

In the session led by BJ Lownie of Strategic Proposals, only about 15% of the 75 companies represented acknowledged that they regularly benchmark their proposal quality and proposal department's capabilities.

Since benchmarking is such a powerful tool to help raise win rates, I'm devoting this article to explaining why this should become a regular practice for all serious competitors in the government market.

Benchmarking proposal department capability

Needless to say, as the government market shrinks, only the best competitors will prosper, and those with high-performing proposal organizations will lead that charge. I have written numerous articles about creating high-performing proposal organizations and how to benchmark your company's capabilities against our industry best practices model (see my article *Here's how to raise your win rate by 20 percent* along with our 7-factor survey results and webinar replay).

You can perform this benchmarking internally, or you can use a professional proposal expert to do the benchmarking for you. However you decide to do the benchmarking, you must create a roadmap for improvement and identify:

- Areas where specific investments should be made.
- Timing of these investments.
- Expected payoff from each investment.

In many of our recent benchmarkings of government contractors' proposal department capabilities, we observed multiple common deficiencies:

- No defined capture or proposal management process, and in cases where a process was defined, nobody followed the process—resulting in ineffective and inefficient proposal development.
- No measurement of capture or performance metrics and no attempt to optimize processes to raise win rates.
- No investment in proposal tools or collaboration tools to provide suitable infrastructure within which to manage capture and proposal activities.

- Insufficient proposal resources to meet workload demands and inadequate proposal training for overworked staff.

- Inadequate decision-making when qualifying deals for pursuit and inconsistent bid/no-bid decisions.

- Inadequate resume, past performance, and graphics libraries to archive reusable documents.

- Overstaffing proposals with too many resources as well as understaffing proposals with too few qualified resources.

Each of these deficiencies is readily apparent when benchmarking proposal department capabilities against an industry best practices model. You can easily develop and implement a roadmap for improvement to address these deficiencies.

Benchmarking proposal quality

I've also written about benchmarking proposal quality (see my article on *7 steps from good to great proposals*). When benchmarking proposal quality, your company should select several proposals to benchmark. When selecting proposals to benchmark, consider those that were generally some of your company's best proposals, but for some unknown reason were not winners in their competitions.

For each proposal, gather up the RFP and amendments, submitted proposal, and any proposal revisions. The review should include the technical, management, and past performance volumes/sections, and any proposal attachments. Don't forget to make the price proposal part of the benchmarking review.

An independent proposal expert, and not someone who is part of your proposal department, should perform the benchmarking assessment. For each benchmarked proposal, you can expect to receive a written report summarizing the high-level findings, recommendations that can be applied to all proposals to improve proposal quality, and an annotated copy of the proposal with detailed comments to substantiate the observations and recommendations. Additionally, insist that your company's leadership be briefed so the independent proposal expert can directly address their questions about how to improve proposal quality.

Some of the deficiencies that we observed while benchmarking proposal quality include:

- Proposal compliance and responsiveness was inadequate.

- Customer understanding was not conveyed in the proposal.

- Proposal was all about how great the company was versus what the company was going to do for the customer and how the company was going to do it.

- Proposal focused on *what* was to be done versus *how* it was to be done.

- Proposal presented few features and benefits—making it impossible to find and score proposal strengths.

- Information was not conveyed clearly—so readers missed the content.

- Solution development was non-existent.

All of these problems are process problems that companies can remedy by training, improving processes, and following standard procedures. As each of these problems is resolved, win rates will move incrementally higher.

Best Informed Wins
Collected Articles of Bob Lohfeld from
Washington Technology (2010 – 2012)

With winning becoming paramount for companies, spending a few dollars on benchmarking to improve proposal quality and capability is certainly a sound investment and will pay off tenfold once improvements are made.

WashingtonTechnology.com, December 12, 2012